MW01169361

# The Closet Channeler

# The
# Closet Channeler
## A Guide to The Light

Heather Hunt

© 2013 by Heather Hunt

All rights reserved. Up to 300 words may be quoted
as long as proper credit is given and a copy of the
publication is sent to the address below. Otherwise,
no part of this book may be reproduced or utilized in
any form or by any mean, electronic or mechanical,
including photocopying, recording, or by any
information storage and retrieval system without
permission in writing from the publisher.

Heather Hunt
P.O. Box 270003
Louisville, CO 80027

Cover photo:
"The Frame"
© 2013 by Heather Hunt

All interior illustrations:
© 2013 by Holly Hunt

Dedicated to all of
my bothers and sisters of The Light.
Most especially my loving and supportive family
and my bright little star, Kendal.

# Acknowledgements

I would like to thank my sister, Holly Hunt, for all of the beautiful interior illustrations she so diligently put together. It was a pleasure working with you and combining both of our visions for the concepts we were presented. In addition, thank you for your companionship, inside jokes and helpful examples (included in chapters five and nine). Love you, lil' sis'!

To my mother: thank you for your help editing "this beast" and sharing your daily insights to your channeling world. It's been an incredible transformation over the past year and I look forward to what you will bring to other's in the near future. You have an amazing gift, it's time to share it. Thank you for everything that you have taught me, your patience and love. Love you, Mom!

To my father: thank you, thank you, thank you, for being so supportive of all "the wacky stuff'" that your girls have been doing in this past year. You are truly "the rock" of our family and I can not tell you how much I appreciate all that you do for us daily. Love you, Dad!

To my daughter: thank you for always reminding me to play and enjoy life every single day. You are my greatest treasure. Love you forever, Baby K!

Megan Beytien, Laura Kraus, Jamie Singer, Julie McMillen, and Jamie Wilding. Thank you all for being supportive, loving and close friends throughout the years - it has been an adventure.

To the one's that do not know how much they mean to me: Wayne Boss, Donn Hayes and Curtis Sears. Donn, you're advice did not fall on deaf ears; thank you for all of your helpful insights.

To all of the channelers before and those after, thank you for paving the way for others and myself.

Last, but certainly not least, to "Devon and The 27" for being so loving and patience throughout this process. I can't wait to see what else we will be bringing forward in the future and the transformation this work will have for others, as well as myself.


Thank you to all for sharing your Light,
Heather Hunt

# Contents

# The Closet Channeler

# Preface

My guides have asked that I share some information on how I work through the concepts they have presented and share notes to my discoveries along the way, as well as, my perspective of the experience of writing this book with them. To begin, while channeling almost every morning and evening for a little less than a month I would often times forget the information they had presented. Instead, I was focusing heavily on being the best conduit for them and bringing the information through as clearly as possible. It wasn't until I started transcribing the book, from the recordings, that I realized the incredible message and detail they were bringing forward. As well as the real energy of the channeling sessions being locked into written word for everyone to experience. My guides and I are very pleased with the final product. Although I questioned them throughout the process and became annoyed with the seemingly repetitive topics and information. I realize after, that the repetition was necessary and helpful to reconnect the foundation topics discussed in earlier chapters to the more dynamic later chapters.

Now, you may be asking, how was I trying to be a better conduit for them? Well simply I would make sure that the information they were bringing forward I could understand. If I can understand it, then I knew everyone else could - we are all One. There are certain chapters where I (and I am sure you) can tell when I was a better conduit than others. For example the chapter: *Source of Light & Love,* the information flowed right through me. In comparison with the *Magnificence* chapter, where I was tired and having a hard time connecting with what they were saying. Also, you may notice there were several times where the guides where coaching me through relaxing and allowing the information to flow. Some chapters came through much more clearly than others; depending on the time of day, diet, health and amount of sleep. My relationship with my guides is very loving, patient and caring. However with that said, sometimes it can be frustrating on both sides. For example when I didn't get enough sleep it was much harder for them to come through. They would have to work with my energy system for ten to fifteen minutes before they could come forward. When I was sleep deprived it was also easier for me to get side tracked and not bring the information forward quickly and accurately. So they would have to resend it over and over again. That is why you may notice that I would get frustrated saying they are repeating things over and over. When, as I said earlier, in hindsight this repetition was beneficial.

While transcribing this book, I noticed the differences between the person I was at the beginning of this book and the person I am now writing this sentence. This material and experience has been incredibly transformative. The total channeling experience took only two months from start to finished transcription of the printed word. This book is a reminder of how quickly we can transform. We are constantly changing and evolving, sometimes it is harder to see than others. With that being said, the past is only a reference point for learning and evaluating where we are today, the future is full of our hopes and dreams. We can not live in either - we must Love today, be present, be in the now and this will better the next moment.

Another of my struggles through this process was learning to trust. Trusting in the process, in the information coming through, in their vision for this book. In the very beginning, I asked over and over again, "is this all being said by me? Why are you having me talk, when it should just be you guys?" Structuring, in my mind, that the book had to be the same as Paul Selig's books; where his guides channel directly through him and he comes forward rarely. I had to overcome this fear and I did. Finally telling myself, "who cares if this is just me speaking the whole time. I have always wanted to write a book anyways." As soon as I let go and relaxed, they came through.

This is where I should clarify, this is not strictly a channeled text. My guides wanted this book to demonstrate the relationship between the guide(s) and the channeler. With that being said, you will notice that a good portion of the early chapters I am much more involved than perhaps I should be. There are two reasons for my involvement in this book:

1.    This gives you, the reader, a genuine illustration of my progress with channeling. Which will provide you with an honest idea of some of the challenges you may face in your own channeling practice.
2.    By having me present some information, my guides were able to conserve energy for more dynamic topics presented in later chapters.

Some advice for those of you channeling or thinking of channeling, you may be asking, "how do I become a better conduit?" My answer: drink tons of water. This may seem strange, but this is the way your guides conduct their energy and messages through you. After a channeling session you should feel uplifted, full of energy, at peace, happy etc. and perhaps a little thirsty - drink more water. Other tips: be open-minded and relaxed. Sometimes I would try to steer the conversation or chapters into the mold I wanted them to fit into - especially in the beginning. But once I loosened up and trusted the material coming through, it became much easier for my guides to come through me and give more powerful information. Also, don't force anything. Let yourself be in the moment enjoying the experience, trust and have fun.

# Introduction

My story begins in March of 2012, when I separated from my high school sweetheart and the father of my child, ending our five year relationship. It was a time of great transition, as a new mother and a recent graduate from college. I made it through the last difficult months of college, one day at a time, with my head held high. I was worth something - I had graduated. After graduating, I didn't know what I wanted to do with my life. Asking myself, "which directions was right for me? To be a stay at home mom, working part-time? To search out my career? To get married and start a family or stay single for the rest of my life?" During this time I was doing a lot of soul searching. Overwhelmed with the feeling of being lost and wondering what my purpose was while here on this Earth. Little did I know, I would receive my answer four months later in the Southwestern town of Sedona, Arizona.

Months before this scheduled trip, I had a pressing feeling that I needed this vacation. I had to go. I had to make it happen, no matter what was going on in my life. There was this invisible force telling me to go, go, go. So the three of us - my mother, daughter and myself - packed up my 4Runner and drove through Santa Fe, New Mexico and into Sedona for our week long vacation. Nothing particularly exciting happened for the majority of the vacation. I noticed I was drawn to the Native American culture, more so than usual. But I dismissed this as being in the Southwest and surrounded by tourist shops, filled with these stylized items.

As our second-to-last day drew upon us, the two of us decided to take a stroll with my daughter around the main shopping drag. Hoping to find something special to take home with us. We walked along, in the heat, making our way back to our hotel. Finishing up a long day of shopping, when my mom uncharacteristically decided to dart into a rock and crystal shop. I followed with slight curiosity and a quiet feeling of annoyance due to the heat and hunger. As we looked around the shop, a very nice lady working behind the desk came around to take a peak at my daughter. You know, the usual, make faces and cooing at the baby - I was used to this by now. My mom and I politely conversed with the lady, eventually turned into the woman asking if we wanted to get a psychic reading. My mom and I both looked at each other a little taken aback. Even though we had expressed interest in getting a reading prior to embarking on our shopping trip, we hesitated due to our Catholic religious background. Here it was, the opportunity, right in front of our faces. Before we could answer, she whisked off to grab one of the available psychics.  She happened to be a jolly Native American woman, who on first impression exuded psychic energy. Both my mother and I knew that she was the real deal. We could sense it, feel it.

As we entered the reading room, we were greeted by an array of rocks and crystals placed in a circular fashion on the reading table. I instantly became a little more cautious, this looked a little witchy. But the money had been paid and I was going to sit through this no matter the outcome. As we made ourselves as comfortable as we could, she told us her story. She had known of her psychic abilities as a child. But because other children didn't express the same abilities, she repressed her gifts. Up to the time of embracing her psychic abilities, she had gone through two near death experiences. I found this especially interesting due to the similar story-line of Betty J. Eadie in *Embraced by the Light*, which had fascinated me since a young teenager. She continued to assure us further, by saying she was a third generation Medium and she spoke with her spiritual guides. To which my mother and I both nodded, not knowing what she was talking about.

Well there it was, time to begin our reading. I opted to go first, knowing my mom would need time to process everything that had just been said. So with the decision made, she began. My mother and I were shocked by her detail and level of accuracy on information no one could have ever known. After our fifteen minutes each, my mother and I emerged from the room with dried tears on our faces and a new sense of knowing. We had just been awoken to a new world that had somehow been lost over the years. We knew that we had purpose and there was more to this world than the hum-drum life we had been living. She left us with some final words on rocks and crystals that help us in our lacking areas (my throat chakra needed some help). She also asked that we pursue reading *The Secret* by Rhonda Byrne.

Once we got back to the hotel we were consumed with thoughts and discussions of what had just happened. On our way back to our Colorado home we stopped in Taos, New Mexico to see the native Pueblo dwellings. I was struck by how naive I had been, thinking that we all lived in the same conditions in the United States. All of these thoughts swam through my head on our long drive back home. After arriving home, my dad instantly noticed the change in both of us and jokingly asked if we had been to a psychic, to which we waited several weeks before answering. When we finally answered that we had; he was surprised by our answer. At dinner that same evening we shared our experience with both my sister and him. The family dynamic positively shifted and they jumped on board: reading spiritual books, writing down dreams, using *The Secret* and exploring different religions. When finally, my mother brought home a book that unlocked the key to my psychic abilities, *Opening to Channel: How to Connect with*

*Your Guides* by Sanya Roman and Duane Packer.

After reading this straight-forward guide on how to connect with my spiritual guides, I was blown away by what I discovered. I had not one, but a collective of twenty-eight different guides. Who made themselves known to me as, "Devon and The 27." I spent the next three months conversing with them about different personal matters and receiving advice. They kept telling me that I needed to open up to verbally channeling. Which after reading Paul Selig's, *I Am The Word*, and watching a YouTube video of him verbally channeling, I said, "no, thank you." I was not about to be the person sitting in the chair, making strange faces, waving my hands around and rocking back and forth, no matter how awesome the information was that I could bring forward. After a month of being bombarded and trying to stay "normal," my mother said her guides had expressed a need for me to verbally channel, as well. So, fine! I would do it. I walked into my closet, where I had been channeling, so as not to wake my daughter. I sat down, opened all of my chakras and gave my guides permission to come through me verbally. No sooner did I say "yes," and they said go. The first session was around forty minutes with incredible information, mostly personal, and most importantly that I would be channeling a book for the world, shortly.

Five days later, we started on the book you now hold in your hands. Taking only two weeks to channel and another six weeks to transcribe. Towards the end of the two weeks I was channeling in different accents and voices. The four in particular included: the collective's rough voice, Devon's Eastern Indian voice, a guide's Jamaican accent and another's soft womanly voice. Here they would like me to explain how the book is written. The guides repeat words several times throughout the book. They have told me this is to get the reader and myself in alignment with the frequency they are bringing forward. Because of these different voices, the text has been marked for better understanding: *italicized* represents my voice; standard, my guides speaking directly and **bold**, represents my guides and I speaking simultaneously. My guides have asked that I translate their channeling into text that excludes standard grammatical practices; capitalization is only to occur with specific words from this point forward. when asked the reasoning for this, they answered, "it will better bring forward the message of this text by not complying with the standards of this world, but rather with the energy of the next."

my guides have asked that i share these final words before the book begins:

this book is written for all of the children of The Light - my brothers and sisters. may we find The Light within and spread this message to others. many of the people in my generation are at a time in their life where they are looking for an escape. an escape from the economy, responsibilities, expectations and needing to be successful. most of us want to run away and get lost in partying with friends and loosing ourselves. we think that we have to be these perfect beings, we have to achieve all of these goals by a certain time or we aren't worth anything. this book is for all of you. everyone that feels lost and worthless, to remember your worth. remember that you are a being of The Light. you are infinite and you have so much potential and power at any age to achieve things beyond your wildest dreams. let this book be your adventure of yourself. once you become in love with yourself and your life, you become at peace and in love with everything and everyone around you. it starts with One. choose your Light and everlasting Love.

# Chapter One

## Choices

Morning of February 22, 2013

we are here, we are here, we are here. we are ready to talk today; we are ready to begin this book. we are excited, we are excited, we are excited. just as you are, just as you are, just as you are. this is good good good. we are glad that we will be able to combine both of our energies and come through you and this is exactly what we want. this is exactly how we want the energy of the book to feel. this is exactly how we want everyone to feel when they read this book - excitement, excitement, excitement. that they are ready to read this story, this novel, and they are either ready to take their own journey or they are not. this is up to them, this is up to them, this is up to them.

today we want to talk about choices - choice, choice, choice. everyone is in their choice, everyone can choose. just as you have chosen to channel us today. you could have not channeled if you wanted to. you could have sat around, you could have slept in, you could have decided, "oh no. instead i am going to shower." but no, you decided to channel - you chose. chose chose chose. everyone has choice. you can all choose to do whatever it is you want to do in this world and we want you to know this. we want you to allow yourself the freedom to know this, "you can be whoever you want to be." and this is powerful. you can choose whatever circumstances you want to live in. we understand that people look at their current circumstances and situations in the past and they define themselves by that and this is wrong, wrong, wrong. we want you to define yourself by who you are - internally. not the future, not what could be, not this, that, the other thing. but we want to define you, we want you to define yourself, by who you are internally. the person that is the inner person. the inner-self. the higher-self. what you want. what you dream about. what you are here to do on this earth. everyone has a purpose - everyone. and we don't think that anyone's purpose is minute. even if it is seemingly minute to someone else that accomplishes - oh conquering a continent or **like uhm columbus finding a new world versus the person on the street that shows one act of kindness that changes another person's life forever.**

this is what we are talking about: everyone has a purpose. everyone has meaning to their life. everyone has a reason why they are here and we want you to cling on to this. we want you to know this is true and we want you to feel this. you can be whoever you want to be; whoever it is, your true self. (devon's voice) "know thy self," is what your mother said this morning heather, or last night, and we want to discuss this. knowing thy self is very important. it is more important than anything else that could be said on this planet. you must know yourself in order to know others. you must know what you like, what you don't like, who you are, what you can accomplish, how much power you truly have. your power is infinite. your power is part of God. we are all One. we are all part of God. their is a Christed-Self within you and you must decide to chose Him. when you choose Him you open your doors. you open your world to the infinite possibilities of eternal love and eternal possibilities. you can accomplish anything you want.

so we want you to choose - choose, choose, choose. you choose to allow yourself this opportunity to be in your Father's Light. allow yourself to come forward. allow yourself to be wrapped in beautiful, beautiful, beautiful Light. think of this as a blanket. a very comfortable blanket. any blanket that you have: your most comfortable childhood blanket, the blanket you slept in last night, whatever it may be. allow yourself to fill that blanket with a white Light, white sparkling, beautiful soft loving Light and let it fill you. as you wrap it around yourself and become comfortable, at peace, at One.

you have all had this experience, we are sure, of sitting out in nature allowing yourself to become One. One with everything around you - relaxing. not letting the mind cloud itself with different things that it must do - must get done. especially in this day and age. everyone is so focused on their future, future, future. what one must get done in order to feel like they are successful - that they have made it and this we think is silly. you do not need to be oprah. you do not need to be the president of the united states to be successful. you are all a success. you have all come to this earth. you are all choosing your choices and you are a success in your own way. and we want you to realize this: we are all One and we must come together as One. choosing to be part of The Light and choosing our Love.

yes, anyway let us get back to what we were discussing before. when you are out in nature. yes, when you are out in nature and you allow yourself to let go, to become part of the Oneness. to become part of the earth. to become part of the air. to become part of the nature around you and the energy of this place. the energy of the universe. you are allowing yourself to become One. yes, feel this feeling. allow yourself to go out in nature and practice this. go out in nature: whether it be the middle of winter. whether it be spring, summer, fall. allow yourself to go out in nature and either sit down or if it is too cold allow yourself to walk around and focus on all the beauty that is around you. all of this - because this is all part of you. and we want you to realize this: you are all part of One. you are all part of the earth, you are all part of the sky, the stars, the trees, the animals, the plants. you are all One.

so you hold yourself away from the people around you. you say, "oh, you are not like this person...oh, I could never be like that person...oh, no. no. no. i do not like what i see there with that person." and that's okay we understand that is discernment. but you are not separate from each other. you are all part of One. you are all together. and this is a concept we are seeing as very hard to portray to everyone. but your brothers and sisters are all around you and to hold them outside The Light is wrong. you are all together, you are all One. And this beautiful earth holds you all here. so we want to slowly allow you to drop these feelings, these barriers, these walls, these, "I am not like the person next to me. I have nothing in common with them." well guess what - you do. you are all One. you have everything in common with everyone else and they have everything in common with you. now think on that for a minute. if you want to stand in yourself, rather than in your ego. this will be easier for you to understand. everyone on this planet has something in common with you. yes, everyone.

now think on that. no. you are not different from the

person that stands on the corner that deals drugs. you are not different from them, as you want to say that you are. they have some aspect of you, they like you and you like them. you choose to do different things. and this is where we want to show you: what you see out there that is different, that makes you separate are choices. but The Light, The Light inside people. this, this is all the same. you are all One. and once you realize this. once you realize that you are all part of the same creation. you learn to forgive. you learn to not judge - this is not your place. who is it for you to say that the person on the corner dealing drugs is not part of you, is not part of the brotherhood, part of the sisterhood, is not part of this creation around you? that you say you are apart of. who is it for you to say that they are not a part of it as well? so do not allow others' choices to affect you. do not allow them, to make them feel as if they are not part of you, as if they are not part of the Oneness around you. because this is not true. we are all One. and now it is time to become One.

so yes we have said that you hold others outside of The Light because of choice and this is true. and sometimes you hold others outside of The Light because of fear. you do not want to seem like your brother. you do not want to be associated with drug addict on the corner. you do not want to be the person that murders someone else. you do not want to be associated with the person that believe in this politic or that politic, or this religion or that religion, or this, that and the other thing. because you do not want to be that person and we understand this. so part of this is fear and part of this is discernment. discerning between others choices and deciding what is best for you and we understand that. so we are saying what we want to get rid of is the fear. the fear that you will be someone else. do you think that princess diana believed that she would be like people that lived in poverty with different ailments. which people usually want to disassociate themselves with - no she did not. because she could not be. you cannot be associated with the person that does this, that, or the other thing. because that is not you and that is not them. that is only an aspect of the life that they have chosen while here or in re-incarnation. you must realize you are all part of the Oneness. your inner-self is a thing that is part of The Light, is part of God. is part of the blanket that surrounds you that makes you comfortable; that makes you feel warm and fuzzy inside and full of Light. you are part of that and so is everyone else. so do not worry about these things that you could associate with. do you think, "oh man, if i associate with them i will become them." this is not true. you already are them. you will not become part of their choices unless you chose to be.

so we are all in choice and this is what we are trying to say. we are all in choice. choices define you. this is something that heather said once. she said, "choices define you." in this way, this is very true. your free will, your choice, your choice to stand outside of The Light, your choice to do drugs, your choice to do the murdering, the killing, the holding your brother outside of The Light, the suing - this is all choice. and this is usually born from fear. and we do not want this anymore, we don't want this grid of fear, as we have explained previously, (to me in my first verbal recording, not in this book) it is like a black net that has swallowed this world. has swallowed this plane. needs to be lifted and as it is lifted, it will be lifted with everyone's Light as they come together. and this world will be blanketed. as you are now, blanketed with a beautiful white Light, loving Light, coming through everyone and they will show this to everyone. and this is what we want you to realize: everyone has a purpose, everyone has meaning. so do not look down upon your brother, who are you to do so? i am sure if you look at your past history

there are things that you are not so proud of. choices that
you have made that you are not so proud of. so do not
allow those to define you anymore. do not allow the things
that you have done in the past to come into your future, to
come into your now. define yourself by your inner-self, the
you that is within. know thy self. come into yourself and
know who you are and we will help you do this, if you so
choose. you can call on any of us here, today, that you are
hearing, that you are reading, that is coming through you
in frequency. you may call on us at any point in time. to
allow the veil of fear that has come over you to be lifted. as
it is lifted, to allow yourself to become part of The Light,
the Oneness, the beauty, the nature, the world, part of
your brother, part of your sister. yes, we want you to do
this. you may choose to not do this. this is up to you. again
we do not want you to feel as if we are coming and we are
saying you must, you must, must, you must. no. you have
choice. you may do whatever you choose. is it for your best
interest? is it probably for your best choice to choose The
Light? yes. but again, this up to you and this is not your
time, if you do not feel comfortable with this information. if
you do not want to choose this now, that is fine. you do not
have to. at some point you probably will. if not, you will
have other lives to choose in. we are not saying that you
must do this. this is up to you. this is choice. if this
resonates with you, as it should. your inner-soul, your
inner-self, then choose it. allow the veil of fear to be taken
from you and instead wrapped in a beautiful white blanket.
allow this. allow, allow, allow. we want you to do this, if
you so choose. allow yourself again to be wrapped in this
white blanket, if you have not chosen before. allow the
warm comfortable feeling of Love, that feeling of warmth,
feeling of Light, feeling of forgiveness, feeling of Oneness
with everything around you and allow this to come over
you. allow yourself to feel the blanket, its weight, its

lightness, all in one. to come through you, into your auric, into your body, into your mind and into your spirit and allow yourself to relax into this.

what we see, is that most people here in the united states do not take the time to relax. they are like busy bees running around looking for their honey and by honey we mean money. focus focus focus on prosperity, focus on achieving achieving achieving that next level, that next level, next level. well guess what everyone. this is the next level. allowing yourself to become part of everyone around you. allowing yourself to be the true you, the inner you, the Oneness with God. allow the creative-self to come forward. for some people like heather it was to start painting again, to start problem solving, to allow herself to come forward with different things she wanted to do and do them. the most creative, the best way she could possibly do them. yes, and she has a project now that she is working on that will inspire many. but this is not why she is doing it; she is doing it for herself. she is doing it for her Love of other people - her Love for the world, for her brother, her sister, for the ancient wisdom, for the truth. the truth that is here on this earth, that is sometimes hard to see. but she wants to convey that. and that is why she is doing her things. and we want you to do the things that you want to do. **the creative-things, the inner-self, that speaks to you. that wants so badly to build a car, to take workshops on how to do metal working, to start blowing glass, to start helping people and allow yourself to go into the non-profit sector. to allow yourself to create t-shirts, create clothing-lines, to solve world problems, to network with people, to counsel them, to help.** because that is what most of you are here to do - to help. to help your fellow man achieve The Light.

so we want to leave you today with this information: that once again, as a recap, we are all One. we all choose or choose not to do the things that we want to do, the things that will help us bring forth our bright, wonderful Light, that allows us to become One. choice is always there. you may choose to connect with this information, you may choose it and then the next second you can choose that you do not want it. you do not want this information in your life, you do not want part of the Oneness. we are all in choice. so we want to leave you today with: what you choose will define you, what you choose will define the person that you feel that you are. and it will define what you feel with other people. whether you are separate or not - you choose this. you choose judgement, you choose fear, you choose and we hope you choose The Light. so this again is all up to you. another thing we want to leave you with is that the veil of fear that has come over this whole entire world is up to you and everyone here, and we are speaking to heather, to lift. to show the inner Light, to work with it. and allow others to see that by becoming beacons of Light, that they connect with this vibration and they can then choose to become One. become part of The Light and give that gift to their brothers and sisters, as well as, themselves.

we want to leave you now, today, saying thank you for the information that you have received into your auric field today. that you have allowed yourself to take in. whether you have accepted it or chosen it or not. we are glad that you have read this part of the book. we are glad that you are allowing yourself to at least see, see the true ability that you have and then it is all up to you to choose or not to choose. know thy self. and now we are going to end this transmission and we will start this evening, if you choose this heather. thank you for your time and thank you for everything that you have done with us today. we love you very much. now go about your day and spread your Light. *amen. name of the Father, Son, Holy Spirit. amen.*

# Chapter Two

## Stuck in Choice

Morning of February 23, 2013

we are ready to begin. we have much to say to today. we are allowing us to filter through you and then come out as well. so this is going to be an interesting thing. we are going to see how you can handle the information coming through you without trying to over analyze it. so some information will come straight through your head, you will feel it coming up the top and then coming out and this is because we want to you to be able to interact with the information that we are saying today - and be able to add your own insights - your own thoughts into it. that way we can see which way you would like to take this information and how others may choose to do the same thing. *"sounds good, guys."* let us begin. we want to continue with choices. we want this information to come come come.

(pause and adjusting here)

we want to continue with choices as we said before. we want this information to come through you and then be processed instead. this is new for you, so you are trying to figure this out, you are trying to figure out how to process this information. allow it to come in through the psyche, analyze the information, allow it to come straight out. well this is how you are doing it right now - this is good, this is good, this is good. *there okay, I just feel like I am really deep right now and i just can't really process all the information - so bring it straight through.* this is true in some ways. yes, but you will be able to analyze it before it comes through. you are still being able to look at the information before it comes out of your mouth. where as before we were coming straight through you - there is a difference. *okay, well let's get going on the book then.* let us begin.

we want to talk about choices. *please resend that.* we want to discuss this today, as we did yesterday. choices will define you, is where we left you off. we want you to realize they will define your past, they can define your future. it depends on what you choose to do, it depends on your choice again. we are not saying that your choice will define you for the rest of your life. in some cases you may think that it will depending on how severe the action is, how severe the choice is. you can choose to move outside of these previous choices. you can choose your Light. you can choose your Divinity. you can choose your true-self and you can allow your beacon of Light within you to shine at any point, at any time. everyone has this. everyone has this. everyone has this. everyone has this. so we want you to realize that you can do this: that you are not stuck with the choices you have made or the choices that you think you are going to make in the future or your habitual choices that you make. so we want you to realize this: you can move beyond where you are now and choose, choose, choose, choose, and we want you to realize that those choices will define you. you can always choose to define yourself by the here, the now, this moment. this is what we are saying to you.

so we want you to realize that every thing can change; in a split second you can change your whole entire life. you are not stuck as most people feel. they feel that they have to go to their job. they feel that they have to do the things that they do not want to do. constantly, constantly, constantly. and this is not true. this is an out-picturing of what your thoughts in your head are. so you are seeing the things in your consciousness out there in the real world. and so this is actually a really great thing. you can look at things and decide whether or not you want to choose them. whether or not you want them to continue to exist within your life. if you hate your job, it is something you do not want to do, you can choose to change that. you have every ability. you are saying, "oh well i have bills that i have to pay. oh well this and i have that." there are multiple different ways of getting out of a job or getting away from something you do not like and choosing to do something that you do like. for example: heather is thinking of someone right now that she knows that is in a job that he doesn't like because of the insecurity of the job, it doesn't offer very much. so she says to him, why don't you go ahead and start something on the side. *you can always start something on the side. something that you are passionate about. something that you have love for and guaranteed this thing will spread; this thing will be successful.* **because other people will feel the energy of love that you have for the items, objects, work, whatever it is that you are doing and they will be attracted to it.** so you understand this is how it works. the law of attraction. people come to things

that other people are in love with, because they want that
love in their own life. they see the energy that goes into
something and want that energy surrounding them.
reminding them of the love that they really have. so we
want you to realize this: success as it is defined in your
society is all about titles, in a way. it's: i am a ceo of this, i
am that, i have accomplished such and such, i am a
business owner, i own this, i own that and this isn't really
true. we are just telling you that success is what you feel it
is - success is how you feel. do you feel successful when
you are the ceo of a company because everyone else says
that is what success means? well then if that is what it is,
then that is fine. do you love it, though? ask yourself this
question: do you love your work? do you love what you
do? do you love the energy that you are putting into
something on a daily basis?

yes, we are saying that you are thinking of all these
little microscopic minute tasks, that you don't like to do
like hmmm...going to the dmv, going to this thing, the
other thing. you don't like doing those things, you don't
have love for them. but in a way that is an out-picturing of
your thoughts and how you feel. you can change that at
anytime. you can choose to allow yourself to love every
single minute, every single day and this will change what
you think and what you see. if you love everything for
what it is and you allow yourself to see the true beauty in
everything. guess what? you will. and everything will be
beautiful and everything will be simple and nothing will be
a drag or a drain on your system because you won't allow
it to be. yes, again, this is choice. you're choosing to see
things that you had to do everyday as bad, in most cases.
instead allow yourself to see it as good. allow yourself to
play with it. this is discussed in *the secret* by rhonda bryne
and we are saying that this is a good read for anyone. it
allows you to see the law of attraction and get familiarized

with it, watch the movie if you want to, whatever you choose. but you can see that if you watch this movie and you allow yourself to see that there is power in love - in giving yourself what you want. which is love through the act of doing something. you will receive love in return. you will see only love out there. you will see only beauty. you will see only the things that you want to see and that attracts you. because that is the energy that you are putting out there for everyone.

as we were saying to heather before she started this book, we want you to get excited. get excited, get excited, get excited. we want you so excited that when this information is coming through you, you are ready. and you are giving off that frequency of excitement, of love, of thrill to be doing something new in your life. and this will be projected to other people that read this novel. we want you to see now that what you are reading, while heather is sitting here in her closet putting this all together; talking through this information and realizing what a transformation she has gone through over a six month period and now she is relaying this information to you. she is ready and excited and you are too. as you read this information you pick up on that vibration. we want you to look inner-self right now. we want you to feel the feelings of excitement. are you feeling as if this information is coming through you, coming through you really quickly and in and out, in in in in and maybe even sticking? you are thinking of the information, you are seeing different images. when you are seeing, seeing them, for most of you that don't know, this is your third eye. this is your creative-self, this is your inner-self working through the images, through the feeling, through the auric field. the energies that you are picking up on, that you are allowing into your system and it is giving you pictures and it is allowing you to move into a different dimension, in many cases. so we

want you to realize this: yes, yes, yes, you are a psychic
being, and we want this to be said, you can choose not to
be, as most people have. they think this because, "oh i can
not be this, because you have to have special education to
do that. you have to have a moment of total enlightenment
to do that. you have to be going to shambhala for your
whole entire life. you have to grow up on the eastern
hemisphere in order to do that." you make up excuses.
excuses, excuses, excuses. you can choose to be whoever
you want to be. you can have psychic powers - everyone
has them. they are just waiting there for someone, or
yourself in this case, to choose.

so we want you to realize this, you are always in
your choice. this world is beautiful - has many mysteries,
has many adventures to go on. unfortunately most of you,
right now, in this modern time are bored. you have stuck
yourself into a job that does this every single day - routine,
routine, routine. you watch shows were everyone goes out
and they go and do all the adventures so that you don't
have to and you allow yourself to be okay with that and
you go, "that's okay. those guys can do that. those women
can go do that, but i cant. i am going to stick here with my
9:00 - 5:00 job and i'm going to go to work every single day
and i am going to support my family (which we think is
great) and i am going to allow myself to be totally bored
and feel totally lost and totally disinterested with life." and
we are saying this is choice choice choice choice and now
we want heather to speak on what she is seeing with this
information. she wants to discuss where she was before all
this, you will have seen this in the prolong written before.
but we want her to allow this information to come through
to you right now at this time as well. so go ahead and speak
heather:

okay. what they are discussing here with the boredom with the lack of self interest, interest in other people, life feeling like it is propelling you forward. i think i had, i know i had a huge problem with that right around the time that i actually met the sedona psychic. and felt pushed by an unknown force to go to sedona and to go there and then to get a reading. it all worked out, it was all coincidental, which in reality there is no such thing as coincidence, lets just say this. you will start realizing this as you start getting higher in your levels and accepting the information into your system. there is no such thing as coincidence. everything is planned. everything has been thought out. everything is methodical: they know where they are going to put you and allow you to open up and choose which psychic abilities you want to do, choose what path you want you to choose. i mean i didn't start off going, "oh, i want to be a channeler. i want to sit in my closet and i want to channel every day." uhmm...i started off with lets watch the secret because that was introduced to us by the sedona psychic. so lets go ahead and watch that. and that was just mind blowing and changed my perspective on life. it gave me a task, a real, inner-task of trying to choose (since we are talking about choice here) trying to choose every single day to love life. many of you right now are like, "okay that is a hard task." and trust me it is, when you go from total disinterest, totally lost, no purpose, to everything is beautiful about life. you have to make this conscious choice effort to improve your outlook and frequency.

yes, i could define myself by: i am a mom, yes i have these roles. yes, yes, yes. but i didn't have a real focus - a real drive. i had just gotten out of college i didn't know whether i wanted to go into real estate, be a stay at home mom, get some random job that would pay the bills or continue working my very part-time job in the mall. but everything changed once i got started on this book. i think i needed the time period, i know i needed the time period of total boredom, total loss of interest and an overall feeling of, "i am lost. i have no idea where i am going in life. i have no purpose except to be a mother, to be a friend, to be a worker bee, to be this that and the other thing," and i defined myself by these roles. by what i though i should be doing with my life and how these roles were supposed to manifest themselves into being the wife, the girlfriend, the daughter-in-law. but it didn't work out that way. these roles that i thought i had to define myself by, because i had a child with my long-term boyfriend, didn't come to be. instead now i have moved on into this beautiful life, where i choose and i choose almost everyday to be in love with life, in love with myself. the hardest thing for me to do at the time when i broke up because i tend to beat myself up about anything and everything. over-analyzing and scrutinizing that, "you did this, you did that and that's why the relationship didn't work out." now i have just chosen that i am going to be in love with me - the real me - the soul that is in there that is going to come forward and i am going to allow myself to be my true person.

many of us are blessed that we live in such a place where we are allowed, and not governmentally controlled or societal controlled, in many cases, to just be ourselves, to be who we want to be. and i am not speaking for everywhere in the world. i am just speaking for the u.s., which is where i live. i am not saying there are not societal or governmental control in other cultures because there are. but then we must all realize that this is an out-picturing of our thoughts and beliefs that these places exists with the, "always have, always will" attitude. instead we must choose to believe that everyone is free, everyone is choosing to love themselves and in doing so love others. we must be reminded that right will always conquer the wrong, that the beauty we see out there is the true-self of everyone coming forward and that yes there are some challenges, but life is coming together. you see this everywhere you go. you see this around you. you choose to see it. people are choosing to move in this direction and maybe i recognize this because i am moving in that direction so must others. i am seeing people now as self-enlightened. watch the reality t.v., watch people in conversations, many my age are asking what sign (astrological sign) are others. people are actually curious. they are talking about it on a consistent level. they are trying to figure out what the future holds. they are trying to figure out what their life purpose is. and they are trying to figure out each other on a deeper level rather than these roles.

**people are very focused on the figuring out the future. future, future, future.** waiting for tomorrow is probably one of my biggest problems. so choosing to stay in the now. right here, right now, i am sitting here channeling. seeing visions, but i am still in myself. instead of project myself into the future and thoughts surrounding the future. which is hard for me. but when i do this. it allows me to relax. this society has nothing but stress on it right now, it has nothing but this achy feeling for tomorrow and what tomorrow will bring. unlike other cultures, mostly eastern. which give themselves time to relax and stay in the present rather than working for tomorrow. after all, this is where meditation and the study of energies originates from - the eastern side of the hemisphere. and they realize that you can not work your buns off every single day working for tomorrow, you have to save some today for you. so choose, choose, choose, choose. this moment right now, this breath here, as you are reading this book. look into yourself and look at your breath and as you breathe in and breathe out feel life, feel you - feel yourself. what is it that you want? what is it that your true-self wants? go ahead ask yourself. go ahead ask yourself, what do i want? what is my passion? and often time it wont be: (if you are a mom like i am) my kids to be such and such, my time spent doing tasks all the time, my time spent making sure that the car gets an oil change. my time spent giving time to other people that maybe don't deserve my time.

even though we are all One, we must choose ourself and our inner happiness as a benefit to everyone else. so what is it that you want? for me it was to help people. it was to have adventure excitement, to reach beyond the self that i had as a facade and reach into the inner me. the person that is in there. that wants to come out. but society says no, or i say no, my ego-self says no and i put myself in a box. so what is it, the things that you want to do? i love painting. i love people, i love relationships, i love forming those attachments and i love to share them with the world. and so that is *why i have my painting line. yes i am sitting her channeling. i am a mom. i go to work six days a week. but i choose, now, to take time for myself. my time for myself is when i am putting together a painting, physically painting and i am in the moment. it reminds me that as i am painting, brushing, i am changing a blank canvas into something that means something to me, as well as others. i am in that moment. i am getting better about this every single day. but i will tell you, choosing the here, the now, if you are like me: type a, stressed about life because you have debt or whatever is going on in this moment that you have basically put into you life (as i understand everything now and you will to at some point). you put all these pressures on yourself and that is kind of hard to understand. that you have chosen that, you have chosen your burdens in life. i want you to realize that if you choose the here, the now, this moment, you choose to find that love for what you are doing. let's say the people that you are blessed to be around: your family, your friends, you if you are by yourself. too much of the time, we do not think about ourselves. you are number one, the universe goes around you, this is not an egotistical statement it is a true statement. your life, your out-picturing, everything that you see, everything that you have in your life, it comes from you. it is your inner creative-self. your energy source attracting everything around you that you see. you are creating everything out there. you are creating everything that you see. everything that you come in contact with. everything, everything, everything. you are choosing it.*

*so staying in the now, you realize the love of now and if you are in love with now. guess what? the next second will be loving, the next one, the next day, the next week, the next year. love love love and beauty coming back to you. because if you don't (and i have done this before) hoping that if i give away everything, all your time and energy, into someone and leaving nothing for yourself. hoping that they will give you back all of your love as you have given them all of yours and emptied yourself - it doesn't work. you are creating, first of all from a place of lack, that you do not have enough love so you will give someone all of yours and leave nothing for yourself.*

you must love the self before someone else can love you. think about it. think about any relationship you have had with someone in a bar, a friend, a family member, that you have given them all of your energy and love coming from a source of lack of love. giving giving giving. hoping you will receive back more. this doesn't work. you can feel it. you feel like you are emptying yourself, as if you are owed something back. they don't owe you anything. no one owes you anything. no one owes me anything. i owe myself what i expect from anyone else and this is true for you.

this is something that is new for me. and is possibly new for other people - to give yourself the time and attention that you expect from anyone else. if you notice the great people out there, the stars, the enlightened people, whoever you want to talk about, they have self-love. and some egotistically but most not. i am not talking about the ego - let's stroke the ego, "oh you are so awesome. you can do all these things. blah blah blah." i am not talking about you looking a certain way that is attractive to many, so therefore you must be amazing inside. no. i am talking about the true-self. allowing yourself to be filled up with Love and Light from the blanket, we talked about previously. this full-of-white-Light-Love feeling, that weight, that comfort and allowing it to soak into the real you. the deep deep you that is in there and choosing this for yourself. and guess what? when you do this, you will receive so much love and attention from others. that you may not know what the heck to do with it. so just trust me, allow yourself to be centered for once.

many people look down on this: you are being the center of your universe and you are allowing yourself to be the focus, rather than this christian value of giving to others. this is true, in the sense, that you must fill yourself up first before others can receive true love from you. this has been talked about in other like books, such as paul selig's, "i am the word." the idea of: i am the glass and that as pure water in, as you are filled with energy and love you can then spill over for others to drink from. this is a great visualization if it works for you. if this does not, visualize something that would work best for you. not everything works for everyone. i know that i had a very hard time visualizing this experience initially. that's when my guides stepped in with the concept of the blanket filling you up with love and sticking with you. this was much easier for me.

that's why there are all different books and ideas. because some people will easily connect with information and others will not. paul selig's book was fundamental to my learning because it was how i discovered that i had the same way of getting my information from my guides, as he did. as i was reading i went, "bam! that guy does the same thing that i do. i just haven't allowed myself to channel openly because i do not want to look like him." which is silly. this is an out-picturing of what i think other people will think about me. i have come to this realization that others will think about me, what i think about myself. if i love myself, they will love me for me. so love you for you. let your freak flag fly. allow yourself to be you. don't be afraid. don't let fear. don't let, "oh my gosh, my grandmother or my son or this person or that person is not going to love me if i am the true me," from stopping you. because guaranteed when you choose you, everyone chooses you. we are all One. we must come together. let's stop this fake facade of who we think we are, who we should act like.

my guides are saying to me here that this does not mean that you should choose the immoral self. which we are saying is always open to choice. but by saying, "let your freak flag fly." is to let go. we have a grip, or at least i did, on life so hard that we can't enjoy any of it. isn't that silly? we go around holding on to things thinking that, "oh if i hold on to this piece, that i think is me, everyone will identify with that." i went through this crisis when i was in high school, just out of high school starting college. where i thought that i needed designer this and designer that, in order to be the greatest next big thing. i will tell you this, filling myself up with nice things was great. some of those things i love and i still have them. but it put me in debt. it put me in a place, that all that i was wearing, all these outer things that i was wearing were who i wanted others to believe i was. which is what a lot of women in our society *do, to project who we want others to believe we are, through these outer things. and it is all based in fear and ego. we want people to associate us with the louis vuitton bag, the coach purse, the beautiful hair, the new manicure, the new this, the new that, the model in the magazine - and this is silly. just be you. everyone will love you for you. i love you for you. is that what you can say about yourself?*

so lets do this, as we are saying, allow yourself a couple moments here. put the book down if you need to. wrap yourself in the warmest blanket you have ever had, so super cozy and cuddly, just makes you shiver when you get into it. because you are so excited, wrapping yourself in that energy of that blanket, soft warm and fuzzy and then lets turn it on. it is this bright beautiful warm fuzzy blanket wrapped around you coming into you, becoming one with you. and it is full of Love, true Love, Divine Love. you should feel this in your heart, right between the chest, as your heart chakra opens up, your Divine self receives this Love. and you see this as a picturing of, or at least i do, of my chest opening up and allowing this bright beautiful Loving light to come in and fill me from head to toe, as i become One with the blanket. the real you. who are you? connect with you. and when you are ready allow yourself to come out. allow The Light from within to come out and now feel the blanket around you. you are two energies together. bonded in love, real love, and relax with this for a minute...*(silence as i do this)*....

alright, so we want to discuss choice. we like this visual, we hope this will help everyone. we hope this will help help help. allow yourself to be loved. allow yourself to feel one with God. feel one with the Christed-Self. feel One with everyone around you. we are not separate, we are not separate, we are not separate. choose love. choose your inner-self. choose to love one's self. and by loving one's self, as heather has said, you will love everyone around you and you will see no imperfections with people. everyone shall be perfect. because the imperfections that were in you, you love. and by loving yourself, you are loving everyone else, because we are all One. and so we want you to understand this, One, One, One. you think that you cannot be forgiven for things, this is not true. you should love every part of yourself. just because maybe, you have done something, that you think you should not be loved for. this is not true, this is not true, this is not true. God loves all. loves all. no matter their choices, He loves everyone. and everyone should begin to love themselves and everyone else. and as they do this they will be lifted into a higher level and the consciousness will become One and this is all done by choice.

so let us say this: what if i do not choose this? what if i do not? you can choose not to. we are going to say to you now, as everyone is moving into this new realm, moving into this new enlightenment, moving into this new paradigm, as it was. it will be very hard for you to continue choosing not to see the things that are right in front of you. not to see the things that are inside of you - the truth. you are loved. everyone loves you. you must love yourself. do not hold yourself outside of The Light. it is within you ready to burst out and spread to everyone. and we will use this example, which has been used in other books, you are a beacon of Light. if it helps, allow yourself to think of a tower, radio tower and you are the beacon of light shining shining shining, or even better, you are the bright light of a lighthouse. your job is to be a beacon to others, to tell them a message, that they are loved. and the brighter, the more beautiful and the farther you reach; the more people can see you and the more people that connect with you, with your energy and realize that they are loved will open up.

and so this is our message to you today: become One. choose this moment, choose right here, right now, to love thyself and then to know thyself. choose, choose, choose. say you will and it will be done. so choose this. and we will continue on with this chapter tomorrow. we thank you so much for your time here today heather. and we are glad that this book is moving in the correct direction. we love you very much. amen.

# Chapter Three

## Love

Late Evening of February 23, 2013

let us begin heather. let us begin. we understand that you are tired. we realize this. we want you to know that we will not take as much time as you think we need, we will only do as we need to. *k what are we going to do tonight guys?* we are going to focus. we are going to begin the next chapter - love. it is going to be about love - loving ones' self, loving others, loving all, becoming One, love love love.

(pause as i reconnect)

　　　we are ready. we want to begin. this is going to be about love. we want to bring forward love into your frequency, bring you to The Light. this is what we want to do tonight. allow yourself to relax, (wherever you are) allow yourself to feel centered. allow yourself to feel relaxed and loved and feel as if nothing can touch you but beautiful amazing love. we have been working with this example of using the cloak and allowing it to come into our frequency and allowing love to come into us. and allowing it to fill us up and then allowing our frequency to fill the blanket up as well and becoming One. One. One with love and this is good, this is good, this is good. we want to continue now, with the thought of love and what it is about. we do not want you to think about love, as it is about, what most people think that it is about in this day and age - which is sex. love is not just sex. yes love can happen during sex. people can exchange the loving frequency during this time frame, but that is not what it is. love is not presents (gifts), love is not receiving all these things, that they think represent love. love is a frequency. love is unconditional. love is when you love an animal or a small child and you love them unconditionally. feel that feeling. allow yourself to think of your most favorite pet when you were a child or a love for a friend, a love for your grandparents. a love for someone that you love very deeply and allow that feeling to fill you up. take a moment now to allow yourself to feel that. lets see, heather is going to give the example now. she is going to go ahead and go with this example. so allow yourself, heather, allow it, allow it:

*my example of this would be that i had a dog when i was younger, his name was Max. he was always a very gentle soul - we really connected. there was some sort of spiritual flow between both of us; he was like my protector. uhmmm...my guy, my good ol' boy, always around, always with me. that is the love that i think of - when i hugged him. he was a rottweiler. so he was pretty big for me when i was a child. i just think of hugging him around the neck and think of feeling the love between both of us. allow myself to fill myself up. especially in the heart chakra, you should feel things within your heart chakra. you should feel it coming into your frequency.* allow it to come in, come in, come in. yes this is very good. *so allow yourself to sit with this for a little while. do not think about, "oh i am going to look silly. what are they going to say next? what is the next example? what are they going to say? do i need to continue reading?" just pause now and allow yourself to take a moment, however long you need, to feel that full feeling. allow it to come into your auric field. allow it to come into your frequency. allow it to attach onto that memory, onto that feeling, and make it now. this is what we are focusing on now now now. choose now. choose this moment, even though it was a past moment, feel the feeling that you did with that person or animal.* and this is what we want you to do. so go and do this. we are going to take a moment for heather, to do the same exact thing that you are doing and then we will come back. so let's pause here.

(pause)

now that you have allowed this into your auric field let us continue. let us continue. bring this into your moment, bring this into your everyday life. this feeling of love is what you should feel for one another. this is what you should feel for your bothers, your sisters, everyone on this planet. and most importantly, we say this, is you should feel this for yourself. allow it into your auric field. allow yourself to be in love with yourself. we are talking about unconditional forgiving love. no matter any of the things that you have done in this world, no matter any of the things that you blame yourself, and any of the things that you judge yourself for or allow others to judge you - you are in control of yourself and you are loved unconditionally by everyone and by all the energy that is part of God, that is part of the Christed-Self, part of the higher being. whatever you want to call it, whatever religious sect you want to name it by, whatever your beliefs are. that person, that energy source, loves you unconditionally and will always love you, forever, for the rest of time. this is so, this is so, this is so. and we want you to realize this. we want you to allow yourself to feel this feeling and know that it is true, because it is true. it is true. and we are saying that, to you today, that you should feel this feeling all the time in your life. and you need to allow yourself to forgive yourself for anything and allow this to come out of your auric field. allow yourself to go through the list of different things that you should not be forgiven for, that you should be judged for, that you are lesser than any of your other brothers, any of your sisters and allow this list to be taken and looked at by yourself. and as you look at it, release it, release it form yourself. put it in a box and tie it up with a pretty bow and allow it to be shipped off somewhere else. allow these things to be removed into, lets say a river. as you look at them, you bless them and release them into the river and you allow them to go down stream to God. allow them to be blessed; allow yourself to move on. allow yourself to feel that feeling, that you are truly in love with yourself, by doing so, you will learn to know thy self. you are in love with yourself. you are in love with the whole world. you are in love with everyone. you do not hold anything against them, because there is nothing to judge. there is only unconditional love, **that feeling that you had with your pet, with your grandparent, with a child, with whom ever the example was that you chose, feel that feeling with, that love, that embrace. that is for the world. that is for yourself. know this feeling and come form this place.**

*when you move from this place. when you move from love, unconditional love, nothing can be wrong. there is no wrong, there is no right. there are none of these dichotomies. all it is, is an out-picturing of yourself and if it is love, well that is beautiful, isn't it? so allow yourself to just love, be loved.* we want this for all of you. we want you all to feel that you are loved, because you are. unconditionally, uncontrollably, you are loved. you are part of the love. you could be nothing else. so you are within this, you are in this, you are in this. so we want you to realize this. move from this place. allow yourself to be this person, that you know that you are. this should resonate with your system. you should want this. you should feel it. **and your ego-self may be looking at this and going, "ahh, i can't love that person that harmed me. i can't forgive that person that made me feel this way, i can't, i can't, i can't and i won't." well there we are again, we are back at choice.** you have the power to choose whatever you want to choose. so choose love, choose it for yourself. choose it and allow yourself to be washed of anything. allow yourself to be cleansed. think of yourself being washed with pure beautiful water, light, fresh, clean water, coming over you and allow this to come into your system into your body and cleanse you.

one thing heather wants to talk about here, is that when we first started channeling through her, we had this session, where we praised her. we are not talking about the ego-self, we are not talking about the person that thinks this, that or the other thing. we are talking about the true her, the inner her, the soul and we praised it. we allowed it to be rejoiced and we said many good things and it was almost like a bath, as we would like to put it, a bath of love. through words, through our vibration. and she was very resistant to it. she will openly admit that. she did not understand why she was being treated this way. she was saying, "i am not God. why are you doing this to me? why are you treating me this way? i should not be treated this way, i am not God. so therefore this is wrong, this is wrong, this is wrong..." wrong. this is right. you are all aspects of the God, The Light, the beauty and you should allow yourself to feel this. allow yourself to know this. to be in your knowing of yourself as love. you are a light, a beacon of hope and beauty. and you should allow yourself to be washed and cleansed in love; and then in return become love and then give love to others. and this is what we want, this is what we want, this is what we want.

it all starts with one and then it moves on like a domino effect. everyone that chooses love, chooses love of themselves and chooses love, therefore, of everyone else. **well, only their world can be full of that. so this must be the same for everyone else's world.** (guides addressing me:) yes, yes, you are going back to the example of aspen trees (discussed prior to channeling for this book) and how their roots are all entwined and they are all one, all one, all one connected together. yes, they may come out of the earth separate. and they may look separate from one another but they are together - combined, combined, combined. they are a network of love, of sharing of equality, of one. so we want you to think on this for a moment. allow yourself to be in a forest, wherever you have been before. maybe you have actually been to a place where there are aspens or you have aspens in your backyard or whatever the case may be. allow yourself to move in with the tree, become one with it, allow yourself to move up into the branches, into the leaves - feel the sun coming into you. allow it to warm you up. and then allow that energy to flow down, deep, deep down into the trunk. down down into the roots and there you find nourishment. not like you did from the sun, which was was warm and full of vivacious energy. but, instead you feel grounded. you feel connected from everyone around you and you feel the nourishment - the cool nourishment of the earth. there you have connected with your brothers and your sisters, as you are above you are below. so we want you to see this: the facade that you have above, that i am a tree alone by myself and i stand alone by myself and i am not connected with anyone or any other thing is wrong. you are as if you are this aspen and you are connected through the roots, through everything, through the surface that you are on, through the ground - you are connected, you are one.

(pause, as i do this exercise)

and heather is feeling this now, she is feeling part of the Oneness. we have been doing many shifts with her energy field today and so she is moving into a higher direction where she will be able to broadcast what we are saying more easily. she will not have to put so much effort into it and she will be able to see things - more easily with her third eye. we are excited, we are excited, we are excited for this to happen. we want you to know this will happen with you as well. we will work with anyone and everyone. we want you to allow us into your field, into yourself. as you read this information, it will have a certain vibration and it will connect with yours or it wont. and this fine, we understand this. you may connect with someone else versus another and this is perfectly fine. your field of energy is choosing what information you want to come in. and what will be appropriate for you; along with your guides help, guiding you. so this book may or may not be what is right for you. we want you to understand this, understand this, understand this. and we love you for it. there is no judgement here; no one judges in this world. you are all loved. you are all One and we see you as that. part of the One, traveling, learning how to become part of that [Oneness] and we will be here to help you in any way, shape, or form possible. so call on us at any time, if you need us and we will help you.

we are ready to end transmission for this evening. and we want to leave you with the thoughts of this: unconditional love, through anyone, anything, anywhere is possible for you, here now, right now, you can choose it. if you so choose, you shall be - love and therefore always loved. let us stop. thank you heather, for your time today we appreciate it. *thank you guys. love you. amen. name of the Father, Son, Holy Spirit. amen.*

# Chapter Four

## Love and Knowing Now

Morning of February 24, 2013

we are here. we are ready. we are ready to begin. we have much to say today. we have much to talk about. lets talk about love love love. lets continue on the path of what we have already talked about.

(pause)

so as the reader has noticed by now. we are choosing to hark back to things that have already been discussed in previous chapters; that way we are laying the foundation for the next chapter. and everything interconnects and everything works as one. we want you to realize this book is part of the circle of One, that all of you are. giving you examples and helping you feel this feeling. it is connected, it is interconnected with all of the subjects on this matter, as you are connected with all the subjects in your matter. so we want you to feel this. we want you to have a love for everything in your matter and love for this book as you read it. we hope that the way we are coming through the energy, that we are [properly] projecting everything. that is, we are saying something that will connect with you, love you and allow you to love yourself, your environment, your matter, and everything around you, as well. so lets us begin today.

(pause)

love is a creation from within. it is a feeling of knowing, it is a feeling of unconditional love. knowing that you are being loved, knowing that you are in love and knowing that everything around you is the same as well. so in a way this chapter is also about knowing. and we want you to know this: **think of an instance, a time, where you felt as if something was going to happen and you knew it was going to happen. and that feeling, should be somewhere in your chest. so think of this example: then allow it to come over you and allow yourself to know this feeling. (pause)** heather is thinking of this now and she has come up with an example. we want her to speak and allow you to hear what this example is:

*mmm...k. it took me a little while to find this example, that's why there was a little pause, and i think this is for everyone. you have to think through, you have to go through all of your categories. so if you can't think of something right away, don't worry about it, allow yourself a moment to relax - in the now. which is what i am learning, and then when you are in the now, you can feel all the things that are around you. your past things and a lot of times you can feel your future and you can feel it here, right now. anyways my example is when you have placed an order on the internet and you know that you are going to receive your package. you're not walking around wondering, "well i don't know. maybe they didn't see that i placed the order and i am never going to get it." no. you know that it is on it's way and you have faith and peace in this knowing. as i think back to this example. i am feeling this knowing in the heart chakra right where the Christed-State is. right were we discussed before. this opening up in the white blanket and allowing it to come into you. you should also feel this feeling of pressure surrounding that area and your gut-feel zone. and that is your knowing feeling - your gut-feel. so that is my example.*

thank you heather. this is very good. yes the reader needs to know this. so that they can connect and they can allow themselves to find their own example. everyone is different, but everyone is the same. so we want you to know. that just because your example is different, does not mean that your feeling should be different. it should come from that area, your heart chakra area, it is a gut-feel. also it can come from abdominal area, hence the gut-feel zone. you can feel it there, as well. so there are two different places that you should be feeling that feeling, **if it is strong enough. then allow yourself to know that. okay this is your Know. this is when you know something is going to happen. you know you are in love.** this is why she was feeling the combination of the heart chakra and gut feel just as she got done with her example in her chest and also down in her upper abdominal area, right under your diaphragm.

so we want you to practice this. we want you to practice working with your knowing. working with your knowing that you are in love. working with your knowing that things will work for you in your life, for you the way that they need to happen. that everything around you is here for you. here now for you to grasp. here now, for you to be in wonder of, in love. **we know that most people have lost this feeling. and we want you to come to this, allow yourself to relax in this. allow this to become part of your auric field and allow yourself to use this on a daily basis. this can change your life and the way you think about things, the way you interact with things, and the way that life interacts with you. so love yourself and love thy neighbor and love everything around you and you will see how much love is returned to you. and you are constantly in love. you can not be separated from this love, as you feel. you are the well of love, you are part of love, you are in love. God is all around you, God is in you and God is here with you - in love, with you at all times. you can choose to move yourself out of the feeling of love, you can choose not to be part of it. you can choose to feel as if you are alone, but you are never alone. we are all One, we are all One, we are all One. so everyone is attached to everyone else, you can be part of this love. so allow yourself to do this.**

we are going to end this chapter on love. we want to go through some of the things we have discussed before. so we want you to know this feeling of love. love is unconditional, love is all around you. as you love others they will love you. as you love your environment, it will become part of love. everything is a reflection of the things that you see inside of you. which is love, love, love. you can not become distant from that love; you can only be more a part of that love. you can choose to not love, but love is always here for you to choose. as you choose love and you are in your knowing state of love; you will see nothing but love that will return for you. and this will be a true change in your life and it will be true knowing of what love can do for you. love is part of God. love is all around you. love is a well that is here for everyone to drink out of and everyone to become One with. love thy neighbor, love thyself and in return you will receive nothing but love. we want to end this chapter with this feeling and this knowing. thank you and we will move onto the next section now.

## Knowing Now

this next section is knowing. and we have discussed this before. knowing thyself and choosing to know thyself is very important. we discussed this in the choice chapter, we have discussed this in the love chapter. so knowing is now what we want to address.

so you already know what knowing means; we already discussed how you can feel your knowing. what it feels like to know that you are in your knowing. knowing is supreme. knowing is part of your energy source. knowing is the feeling, the energy you put out there. that you are in your love, you are in your state, you are in your now. yes. in the now can mean knowing things that will happen in the future, knowing things from the past, that is fine. what we want to say again is be in your now, know that you are in your now. feeling knowing that i am here, right now, i know this feeling. because that is the most concrete feeling that you could possibly feel. this breath here, now, in, out - that is now and that is knowing. you have this time, this moment, this second, to breathe and to know that you are here on this earth surrounded by loving people, loving relationships, loving objects, a loving self and you choose that. so knowing is being here, being here, right now and choosing this now, this moment. we want heather to discuss being in this moment - know now. is what the chapter will be titled - knowing now.

*okay so, knowing now for me is like they said, is knowing the breath. yoga helps teach me the now through breath and movement.*

*also mediation taught me the practice of focusing on the breath to focus the mind to the now. knowing now should be here, this moment. should be this breath, in and out - allow this to happen. take one breath in, one breath out and know now. know now that you are in love and that everything is in love with you. you are in love with yourself and therefore everything must love you. you are in your choice - here and now. you have Divine Will. you can choose your Divinity or you can choose your ego - this is up to you here, right now. you can change your future from this moment, here, right now. you can change your feeling about your past and your past actions and your thoughts and you can change them for the future. here, right now. you have this breath. you have this moment to choose what you want. you can remove any bondages you have to any of your past actions and anything that you feel is keeping you from your love and is keeping you from your choice and keeping you from the here, right now - allow that to melt away. anything that you see that is holding you in chains and holding you down, making you feel guilty - allow that to be moved away. remove those chains from yourself. take an invisible hammer and remove those chains, if it is rope cut yourself free and allow it to move away. allow yourself to become free here, in this moment. allow yourself to be surrounded by nothing but white, beautiful, light. in a bubble shape, if you would like, you can expand it, retract it, you can make it thicker, you can make it thinner - work with this visualization. feel how beautiful your ability is to imagine things. allow yourself to be here, in the here and now. allow yourself to relax in this moment. this breath. (pause as i do this).*

this is very important. if you choose the here, you choose the now. you are not choosing the next second. you are going to this moment. now. and you are choosing to make change. you are choosing love. **you are choosing this moment to allow yourself to become part of The Light, part of the brotherhood, the sisterhood that surrounds you. you are choosing this, by this moment, right here,**

**right now and knowing it.** *and by knowing it, maybe think of this as owning it.* you don't own anything, as we want to say, but maybe this language would be a better term. owning this moment. you own this here, this here, right now. what do you want to do with it? do you want to think about past actions and how awful things were or how this and that person treated you and how things aren't fair? or do you want to think about all the things that you have to get done and you have to get them done here, now, in the next couple seconds or life is going to pass you by? or do you want to think about your future: "this is what i want to do with it, these are my plans, this his how i want to influence life and this is what i want to do?" well guess what everyone. you don't have either one of those things. you do not have the next couple of seconds, you do not have the future, you do not have any control over any of that or you do not allow yourself to break from the past. if you do not allow yourself here in this moment, in this now, to take control and own it. own it in love. own every action, everything you do in love. do everything in love. become in love with yourself, your life. when you do that, you cannot hold onto the past. you can not allow those things to affect you. because they are not who you are. you may think that you define yourself by your past, by your roles, but they are not who you are. so if you know yourself here, in the now. here in the now you have this breath. you have this moment. you have this feeling of life and you can choose to love it. or you can choose to busy your mind with busy thoughts of things that you must get done. different thoughts about the past, the guilt. you can overreach into the future and feel that you have a grasp on it, but you do not. you have this moment. so live every single moment in love. in love. for yourself, for everyone else around you and life will love you back. people will love you back. this world will change into the future you want it to be, because it is nothing but love. so you will love your future and it will love you back.

so this is very important. we want you to realize this today: be in your knowing of this moment and choose to feel in love and know this feeling. own this feeling. allow it into your field, allow it into your system, meditate with this. say to yourself, if you want to, "i am in my knowing of myself in love; with myself and with other people. i am in my knowing. i am in my knowing. i am in my knowing. i choose love. i choose my divinity. i choose to be in love with everything around me. i am in love. i am in love. i am in love." you can choose any chants that you want, as long as, it rings true to you and rings true to this purpose which is about true love. love with oneself, love with others and knowing this moment. so saying, "i am in my knowing of this moment, as being in love with myself and others around me." and allowing yourself to repeat this mantra in your meditation. and feel the feeling, will allow you to move into every moment with your eyes open, working, doing the things that you need to do - as being in love. think of everything as love. that unconditional puppy love - for everything.

*a child is in love. a child is in love with everything. every child is excited about knowledge, is excited about the here, the now, sleeping right now, feeling comforted right now. they do not think of the future. they do not think of the next moment, they feel what they feel right now. i am talking about children from the age of two or younger, since this is all that i have to reference.* so become like a child, again. focus on the here, the now, being in love, in wonder with the world. be in adventure with it. learn form it. and then be able to teach others form it. become a child again. a child of The Light. a child of the Love and choose this. we bless you and we thank you for the work here today and we look forward to the next coming chapters. *amen. name of the Father, Son, Holy Spirit. amen.*

# Chapter Five

# Love Thy Neighbor as Thyself

Morning of February 25, 2013 (lost recording)

while channeling this chapter, i was unable to get it properly recorded. although my guides attempted to tell me several times, i did not realize until the session was over. therefore the following are notes that i took right after the session and my expansion on what was discussed.

this chapter was about loving thy neighbor as thyself. in order to do this, one must love themselves and then the frequency of love will be carried over for others to resonate with. often times we have a hard time loving all people as we should love ourselves, because we come from a place of lack. we think there is not enough love to go around. or we seek to separate ourselves from others out of fear and control. we do not want to be seen as our brother or our sister, so therefore we do not love them. but this is only harmful to ourselves. because we are all interconnected, we are all One. so here is my example to help people to love thy neighbor as thyself.

when you look at another and you see them, see them as not separate from yourself. see them as an aspect of you, as an aspect of The Light. there is an example in paul selig's book, "i am the word," that asks the reader to place themselves in a room where they are surrounded by all the great people in history. for myself i placed gandhi, buddha, einstein, edison, etc., in my room. now, imagine that these people hold all of the knowledge. how would you feel? would you feel less than them or would you run to them and ask them all the questions you could? when i did this exercise, i ran to them and asked all of the questions i could. because it has always been my experience that others are willing to help. now, the guides have you imagine that you are the one with all of the knowledge. how would you feel? superior? or questioning why others believe you know more than they do. why do others not see their own self worth? and then finally you are asked to see everyone as equals, unto themselves, and ask yourself how you feel. please take a moment to do this example, if you would like. then i will tell you how my sister approached this example.

my sister, has always been an animal lover, since the day she was born. she has been a caretaker of almost every type of house pet you can possibly imagine. she is constantly looking up spiritual meanings of animals and queues into these things. well, when she was asked to do this example, she came up with a very unique way of seeing everyone in the room. rather than seeing people as people, she instead saw them for their animal totem. instead of the room being filled with people that knew more than she did or didn't, they all became friendly. each animal in this world possesses good and bad qualities. your dog or cat may possess good and bad qualities - but you love it. you love it unconditionally and uncontrollably. you may not always be pleased with its' choices, its' behavior, but you love it. this is what the guides are asking us to do. they are asking us to take people and love them for who they truly are. overlook the choices they have made and get into the soul of things. this is the only way that the net of fear can be lifted - through love. look at positives in life and in people and then everything will be positive.

*this is one of the most powerful concepts, once you realize it, you are in control. you have the power, yes you, the one reading this sentence right now. you have the power. your brothers and sisters have the power and as we realize this, we are united in the power we will become One. when you think positively only positive things can come into your life. i should clarify, it is not only thinking positively it is feeling the feeling of positivity - love, happiness, laughter, life. when you are sending that frequency out there you can only receive that back. now, you may have times when things aren't going the way that you want them to even if you are being positive and this is because there is a lesson to be learned or there is a better direction. a better Light path that will make your life even more amazing than the one you think that you need to be on. so embrace everything, do not let it get you down. learn and love, these are the two most important things you can do while you are here.*

*        some of you are saying, "well that sounds great and all. but when the guy cuts me off in traffic, you best believe i am going to be sending out a negative frequency there." and to this i must laugh first and then reply. of course there are things on a day-to-day basis that you feel are acting upon you. but i must ask you this question, what did you do to attract that moment? where you upset at someone earlier in the day and so now this action is continuing to allow you to stay in the upset frequency - you have attracted it to you. where you just thinking a negative thought and this is why this moment happened? when these moments happen, look at them, evaluate them, because they are a reflection of your thoughts. think of the world like this, a still pool, where all of your thoughts that you are giving energy and emotion are playing themselves out in the reflection for you to see. they are there for you to evaluate, to conduct and change. all you have to do is change your thoughts, feelings, and emotions to what you want to see out there - in the world - and presto! you will see them.* **we promise, we promise, we promise.** *"be the change that you want to see in this world" (mahatma gandhi). this starts from within.*

*        once you realize that you are conducting your own life*

through your thoughts and feelings you start to become afraid of what you might think next. i am here to say that as you choose love, you choose to no longer be afraid. when i am dealing with negative thoughts, i use the following example: imagine that as these negative thoughts come to you they are placed in a bubble. you look at them for what they truly are, nothing but a thought and you allow this bubble to be sucked away from you. imagine they are being sucked away into a black vortex behind you like a vacuum - cleaning up my mind. as they are sucked away, take a step closer to the bright radiant light ahead of you. give love for that thought, because it is bringing you closer to The Light. feel that feeling of love. radiant. Light filling you. i use this whenever i have a negative thought that just won't leave me alone. when you do this, you are replacing negativity and annoyance with yourself for thinking the thought into love. you are empowering yourself and letting nothing get you down.

let us go back to people and this separation issue. we usually separate ourselves from one another due to others' choices. we do not want to identify with them or place them in our lives. which is good, because we are discerning. but as long as it is only going to the extent of discernment (distinguishing between things without giving them energy). once you cross over into judgement (giving negative energy) you are holding your brother or sister out of The Light while still trying to remain - this doesn't work. you are removing yourself from The Light instead. so this for me is walking a tight rope in my daily life - trying not to criticize, trying not to judge. they want me to give an example here: one of my good friends was going through a messy break up. she was turning to drugs as a solution to her problems rather than resolving them for herself. now of course, i love my friend as if she was my own sister. but at the same time i was watching something happen that i did not approve of, or like. instead of being judgmental, i distanced myself from her and from her issues at the time. now, looking back i wish that i had said to her, in a loving way, that i could no longer stand by her side in support of her choosing drugs. she resolved her own drug and relationship issue shortly after i distanced myself. i still remain cautious about forming a tighter attachment. in the end, i believe if i had approached it a strong loving way and told her, i would have nothing to distance myself from. she may have not changed, but at least i would have removed that energy from my field. what they are saying to me now, if you are coming from a place of love you can do no wrong.

we must realize that we are all here to make our own choices. we may not like the choices we have made, we may not like the choices that others have made. but at the end of the day we must all love one other, we must all choose The Light. we are all One. Love conquers all. we have this beautiful gift of freedom of choice. do not judge others, for it is not your place. they can only judge themselves, just as you can only judge yourself. release this feeling of control and allow others to be as they wish to be - you will be giving this gift to yourself in return. so i challenge you today to think only in positive affirmative ways rather than negative. do not judge others, instead look at their choices and discern for yourself what works best for you. make a conscious effort to stay positive and in the loving frequency. notice how others react to you, notice your drive home and the ease. notice the beauty of this earth as it surrounds you. choose positivity. choose love.

one last thing they wanted me to say. when you are saying negative things about others; you are really saying those things about yourself. would you like it if someone said those things to you? if not, do not say them about others. [your self worth is worthy of more than these words of hurt formulated for others by your ego self]. love thy neighbor as you love thyself. treat others the way you want to be treated. do unto others as you would have them do unto you. it's all elementary material, that if followed, will change your life forever. may The Light be with you. amen.

# Chapter Six

## Knowing Thy Love

Evening of February 25, 2013

we are ready to begin. yes yes yes. *what is it that you would like to do tonight?* we want to start the book. let us continue, let us continue, let us continue. *how would you like to begin?* we want to continue with love. love love love. this is very important, very important, very important. there is much to be said about this concept - much to be said, much to be said. everyone needs to realize that they are loved, that they are from love and that they only can be love. they have never walked away or been out of love, ever, in their lives. unless they so choose or unless they have allowed themselves to become blinded and allow themselves to become swallowed by other things. their love is with them, always, always, always. you are always in love and always in a state of love, if you so choose. allow yourself to do this. allow yourself to become in love with yourself and allow yourself to be loved by everyone around you. you are always in love, you are always part of the Creator, you are always here and you will always be in love. so we want to say this to you: choose love. choose, choose, choose love for yourself and then so choose it for everyone else around you.

allow yourself to let go of anything that you feel has ever been harmful for you from someone else. allow yourself to let go of anything that you think has ever hurt you. allow yourself to move on. allow yourself to become part of the peace, the serenity around you. and this is the easiest way doing it and we will tell you this now. we want you to sit here by yourself and allow yourself to think through any negative thing that you have ever experienced and we want you to wash them away. we want you to wash them out of your system with white beautiful radiant light. you can first surround yourself with the blanket, if you so choose, and allow yourself to be comforted by this and allow yourself to become filled with this beautiful white light. and then as you so choose to do this, then allow every single piece of negativity that has ever been brought into your life by yourself, [we create the negative situations in our lives, not others]. we want you to realize this first, we want you to bring it up to the very top. analyzing it for what it is: usually it is an out-picturing or an internal feeling of fear of being alone, of not being worthy, and this is wrong, this is wrong, this is wrong. you are part of God, you have part of Christ, you are perfect in every way shape and form and there's no reason to judge yourself. you are not the one to judge, you are not, you are not, you are not. you are only allowing these ties to hold you back and hold you away from your Light; choosing to not allow yourself to become one with God and One with everyone around you. and we want you to choose this, choose this, choose this, choose this. so as you bring these things forward, as you analyze them for what they are, allow yourself to release them. allow them to release outside of your energy field and by doing so allow them to be washed away. you can envision this is taking a piece of debris and washing it away from you. whether it is something you visualize as being a black orb or whatever it may be and washing it in beautiful white light. allowing it to slowly sink away into this beautiful white light that surrounds you. and penetrates into your hand and fills you with love, love, love, love. any voids, any feelings that you have of this thing missing from you, whether holes in your energy system or whatever it may be, allow it to be filled - filled with white light. allow this to surround you, as you slowly allow water to come into your system, you'll see the things that have been stowed way deep inside your system will come forward to you. as they come forward allow them to come, do to not resistance them or bury them deeper. allow to come up to the surface and allow yourself to cleanse them; analyzing them and cleansing them.

this is what you need to do this evening. allow yourself to do this and you will become part of One, part of Us, part of God and allow yourself to be filled with Light. Light and Love. love for yourself. you are part of the Divine, you are part of God. you are part of this world filled with beautiful beautiful Light and we want you to realize this this evening. heather is seeing herself with wings behind her back, as if she is part of the angel and we do not mind this is. this is part of feeling as if you are part of The Light, you should feel that you are elongated. you should feel that you are full of Light and beauty and that everything around you is an energy source and an energy feeling. this will mean that you will feel elongated. you feel as if things are tangible, but yet they're not. that you can move through them and they can move through you and everything around you is in motion. the solidity of the thing that is below you, which is called ground - is not solid. you're on a moving axis, everything is moving. everything is moving, everything is moving, everything is energy. we want you to realizes this: everything in this universe is energy. it can be attracted to you and you can choose whatever you want. so choose now, choose The Light, choose this and allow this. affirm it to yourself: "I am choosing The Light, I am choosing this for myself and I am choosing to see The Light in others. I am choosing this here, now, and I will choose it for the rest of my life." you should begin to feel an elongating experience, as you move upward, as you move higher into your energy field and as you become closer with your Divinity and closer with your Oneness. we want you to do this, we want you to do this, we want you to do this. (pause)

this is very a good heather, this is very good, this is very good. continue on this path, continuing and allow yourself to move upward. allow yourself to move upward upward upward. yes very good, very good, very good. we're working with your energy system right now. we are moving everything into where it needs to be. we are allowing you to move upward into another energy field; so we can come into your system more easily and so the information that you are receiving will become clearer to you.

(pause) *what should this part of the chapter be called?* knowing thy love. knowing thy love in thy self. (pause)

alright we must begin. we want to recap this. you should feel a sensation of floating, you should begin to feel yourself as if you are on a cloud, moving upward, moving upward, moving upward - into your Light. surrounding yourself with beautiful Light. allowing yourself to feel this feeling of energy coming into your system and allowing yourself to become one with God and One with everything around you. as you allow the things that you think are impurities, and things that do not belong in your system to remove themselves; to allow yourself to move upward upward and become part of The Light, part of the beauty in everything around you will become One with you. heather is feeling this now. she is feeling this in her system, you should too as well. as you're moving things, you will slowly feel yourself lifting upward, upward, upward, upward...as if you are almost flying, floating, this should be coming over you. If it is not coming over you that is because you're still working on some things that need to be removed from your system. allow yourself plenty of time to do this, come back to this, practice again tomorrow if you need to. allow yourself to move beyond this and then once you do so, you will be able to accept the information moving forward.

we know this is a lot of time and effort placed into this, but this is very important, very important, very important. once you do this, you will be able to move upward. you will be able to connect with your guides, if you choose so. and you will be able to feel the energies from other people, and allow them into your energy field, allow them to pass through you. so that you can be connected with everyone and feel what it feels like to be One. realize that you're contributing to this One and everything that you think, is also what others are thinking too. everything that you are thinking, is coming back to you and it's also in the Oneness. so your positivity and positive thoughts are adding to the positivity of everyone around you and into this world. and this is very important. we want you to realize this: when you think negative thoughts, your adding to the negativity. you're creating a negative field and you're allowing yourself and others around you to feel the way that you feel in a negative response to this life and this is not part of The Light, not part of The Light, not part of Light. we want you to move upward into The Light. allow yourself to feel wonderful feelings of love, beautiful feelings of love. feel yourself in nature, feel yourself with your best pet, and holding your newborn child. feel yourself with your loved one, holding yourselves in an embrace. allow yourself to become part of One. allow yourself to become part of love and allow everything around you to become loved and loved in yourself. this is very important.

we leave this with you tonight and will continue on tomorrow and we will continue and we will allow you, now, to relax and come back down. we want you to come back down, allow yourself to feel as if you're on the ground. allow yourself to sink into the ground, allow yourself to feel connected into earth, into nature. think of yourself as being able to embrace or touch grass, allow yourself to run your hands through it in your minds eye. come back down, come back down, come back down into nature. allow yourself to come into nature, allow yourself to come into the earth. there yes, this is good heather, this is good, this is good. allow yourself to become grounded again. we will leave this example with you tonight my child and we will continue on in the morning. we wish you all the best and we thank you so much for all your time and effort this evening. we will continue with this in the morning. we love you very much. *you too. amen. name of the Father, Son, Holy Spirit. amen.*

# Chapter Seven

## Love and Matrimony

Morning of February 26, 2013

we are ready to begin heather. yes, yes, we are ready, we are ready. (pause) today we want to discuss...marriage and what the concept of marriage is. we want to discuss how it is a part of love. how it is the conception of love. how it creates love. how it can be a form of love. how it can be misconstrued as love and all of these things together - create matrimony.

we want to discuss that matrimony is between two people and when they decide to choose to join together. when they decide to join their lives together. when they decide to join together in sex. when they decide to join together and make a family. when they decide to join together and share their life here on this earth, together, and possibly the next life as well. we want to discuss how this is construed as love. how this is discussed to be love, how this must be love. and this is true in some forms it is love, as long as, the intention is for it to be love and for it to be love on higher level than just physical and higher level than just sexual. many people construe love, as love, as being something that is: what you can do for me, what is the physical attribute of love, what is the feeling of love, as far an in the gut or stomach - this excitement of love. but this is not love. love is when you feel an extreme emotional attachment to something and you feel their spirit, you feel the real them, and you honor them for their true Light, and their true Love, and in their higher-being, their higher-self and you honor them for this. this is what true love is. this is what love is. this is unconditional love. and this is the love that we want to continue to see in matrimony, not the love you find physically in the body.

we want you to see that there is more to love than making kids together. we want you to see that there is more to matrimony, than doing this. yes, this is part of the concept. this is how you make love and you allow love to grow is through having children, as long as, you are doing this in a loving unconditional loving state. which is were you see the other person's Divinity, you see the other person's higher-power within them and you see this, you see this is, you see this and you honor it. when you are in the act, sexual act or whether you're in daily life with them. when you choose to take them into your life, when you choose a marriage ceremony. we are not talking about the legal aspects, we are talking about when you choose the ceremony, when you choose to do it. are you choosing to combine your souls together and combine in an effort, on this earth and on this plane, to be together, in One, in love, in unconditional love and through this what we called marriage. in doing so allow children to come into your life if this is what you choose, as a byproduct of your love. so that they can continue to spread their love, their unconditional higher-loving state to other people, as well. this is what we call the chain of love. now, heather is saying, "well you don't necessarily have to be married to do this." no, no, no, you do not. we agree with this, you do not. you can have children with anyone at any state, anytime and you can choose this, to do this in a state of love. yes, it will not be a matrimonial state and often times it does not turn into that, but that is up to you, and that is your choice. we think it is best, in most cases, to choose a matrimonial state. but we do not think, we do not judge anyone for doing outside of that. often times there is a great thing called love children. we just think it is best for the child if they have their family and parents together and they create love and continue to be in love inside of a relationship rather than outside of it. because otherwise it's construction of love. not that they can't receive unconditional love, at this point, it is just different for them. it creates a different dynamic.

so yes we want to discuss, that we think it is silly in many ways, that people pick other people based on physical attributes. rather than the feeling of feeling love, unconditional love, when they are with the person. if you're not feeling this with this person, we do not recommend that you continue on in this relationship. that you continue on in the matrimonial state with them. we want you to realize, it is very important to feel that feeling when you are with the person you plan on choosing to be with. feel the feelings of being in love. feel the feelings of real, true, unconditional love. and by doing so, then you know that you are with the right partner and they're with the right partner and you're choosing this at a Divinity level. rather that at a level that is physical.

yes, this is the discussion of matrimony that we wanted to have and this is what we wanted to discuss today: matrimony versus physical attributes. so now that

we have complete this...(pause)...so now that we have
completed this we can say we are done. done for today and
we can move onto the next chapter later this evening. yes
heather, you are receiving this information right, we are
ready to begin the next chapter this evening. do not worry,
this was a short chapter, we just wanted to get it out of the
way. thank you for your service. we thank you for your
time here today. we love you. *love you too.*

# Chapter Eight

## Love and The Domino Effect

Evening of February 26, 2013

yes, yes, allow yourself to relax heather. yes, allow us to come into your system. yes this is very good, very good, very good. yes, yes, yes. we are ready to speak today. we are ready to begin more on the chapter. allow us to come in. yes, shift yourself, allow us to come into your system. you will notice that we are working with your ear, (i had an ear infection at the time) we're working with your body. we are attempting to heal you, heal you, heal you. yes we want to re-align you into The Light, into The Light, the bright beautiful Light. open up your third eye now. yes, yes, yes, this is very good. yes, yes, yes, we want you to do this. allow yourself to relax, cleanse your mind. allow it to relax, white Light, white Light, white Light. very good, very good. we are taking you deeper, so that we can come through you more easily. yes, this is very good. hear us coming in? yes, yes, yes, here we go, here we go. yes we

want to begin on this chapter. we want to talk about many
things. we have a lot to say tonight, a lot to say, a lot to say.
let us begin.

(pause)

     yes, yes, we want to begin. yes, yes, you heard us
correctly. we want to discuss marriage. we think it is very
important part of society. we think it is something that a lot
of people want to discuss; a lot of people want to know. a
lot of people want to think on. they want to know about
the subject - especially yourself. so let us begin; we want to
discuss this. yes, it can be a holy union between two
people. two people joined can be something that is very
special.
     yes, yes, yes, you have thought of this right heather,
for your life. you have thought of this as a joining of souls,
as a journey of souls together, together on this earth. and
this is correct, this is correct, this is correct. and we want
you to realize this: so when anyone is taking this step
you're choosing to join yourself together in soul path. so
we want you to do this and we want you to do it right. do
not take this union lightly. allow this to be special, allow it
to be important, allow it to come through you when you
decide to take this step. you do not need to give away your
authority to other people to allow this to happen. you do
not need to get permission from your parents. you do not
need to get permission from the priest. you don't need to
get permission from the state. you do not need to get
permission from anyone. this is a choice between the two
parties and they must choose it and they must chose it in
union - they must choose it together.
     this is also usually a path that has been chosen
beyond, before this point, before they come to this earth.
they are joined together in this way. yes, we are not saying

that people do not join together in improper unions because they felt that they needed to. because they have usually done this out of fear and this is not what we want. this is not what we want, this is not what we want. we want people to join together because they are meant to join together. *"are there people here that are meant to be single?"* yes, yes, yes. there are people that are meant to be single for a part of their life. yes, yes, yes. not everyone has a soulmate completely to themselves, but they can choose one. they can choose to have this experience. they can choose to have whatever they want. so they choose it while they are on this planet. they can do this if they choose this. if they fully claim this to themselves, of course a soul mate will be provided to them. everything can be changed; everything can be manipulated. this is not the word that we would like to use. but everything can be changed into what you choose, whatever the other person wants. if you truly choose this, you choose it out of love and you choose it out of the higher-self and out of higher being - out of a higher good for yourself. and yes yes yes, everything can be provided for you. everything can be given to you and we mean - everything.

so we want to say this to you: matrimony is not something to take lightly; the union of souls is not something to take lightly. we want you to choose this and we want you to choose this out of love, out of true love, out of the union, out of unconditional love love. we do not want you to choose this out of sexual behavior, out of physical interest. we do not want you to choose this out of money. we do not want you to choose this out of outward appearances and outward feelings. we want you to chooses this for the person, the inner-person, the real person. you will know the answer, you will know the answer, you will know the answer. when you are coming to the question of whether not you should marry someone. whether or not you should join with them. you will know the answer. you have the answers. the real true burning desire answer to be with this person, that you know that they are right for you, that this is meant to be and you have this answer. do not question yourself so much, do not question yourself. everyone seems to question themselves. everyone seems to ask, "well what if this? well what if that?" well just follow your true path, follow the true-self, follow that energy. you will reach where you need to reach. you'll be with, who you need to be with. you'll attract the things into your life that you need, in order to follow the way that you were supposed to get through this life and the things that you're supposed to accomplish and the mission of why you were here.

*"does everyone have a mission that is set forth?"* no, not everyone has a mission that is set forth. some choose their mission as they are here. some choose it beforehand. some have it already, chosen for them. this depends, this depends, this depends. not every case is the same. not every person the same. but yet we are all One. we all come together on this walk of life in different ways, in different forms. but we are all One. we are all seeking one thing and that is unity. we are seeking being together, we are seeking this and we want this. we want to feel the beauty, the connectedness that we feel when we are together. when you are not in this life. when you are not in this realm, you feel that feeling. and that is what you want to get on this realm. you want to feel that feeling. and this is why some people feel alone. they do not feel the feeling. well that is because they're not choosing to. you must choose in your system, you must choose to realign yourself. you must align yourself with Oneness, with everything around you - the energy source. you must bring this into yourself. and when you bring this into yourself you will know that feeling. you will feel it throughout you. you will feel energy coming

through you and moving around you. everything flows, nothing is solid.

we want to discuss this tonight: nothing is solid. everything that you think is solid, is not solid. the energy around you, is all moving in a way that is attracted by you. you are a conductor of the things that you see around you. yes, of course, some things come into your life because they need to teach you. in order to move you forward, progress your energy forward. move you into the right place. where you need to go. what you need to do. but all this around you, everything you see, you have chosen - the good, the bad, the ugly, and the most beautiful. and you can change it all. you can have whatever it is that you need to have - you need to have. not always what you want or always that you think that you should have. but what your higher Divine Will needs in it's life to accomplish the things, and the tasks that it needs, while it is here on this earth. you must realize this: you are not alone. energy and frequency is all around you. you can choose to connect with anything. you can choose to connect with anyone. you can choose to connect with your inner Divine-self and everything beyond that. you can choose this, you can choose this, you can choose this. it is up to you. choice again. choice, choice, choice.

so we want you to think on this for a minute. for those of you that have thought that you are alone. that you have thought that you have never been around anyone that has loved you. that you have never been in love, that you can not feel love - yes, you can and you already have. you are the well of love. you are the source of love. love is within you. when you choose to love thy self and choose to come from a place of love, and choose to come from this well of love that exists inside you. then you will have nothing but love outside of you. you will experience nothing but love in this lifetime and you will accomplish love. and you'll give love to other people and they will do the same thing.

we have talked about the domino effect and this is what we're saying. when you give the same energy, people will choose to connect with it or they will not. but they will see in a higher realm and their higher-self can either choose to connect with that energy, which most often times they do and they will spread this. yes, yes, yes, heather, you're seeing this image that you have been told about through betty eadie's book. that everything is energy and when you send out a bad vibration, when you send out a bad vibe, it is like a ripple effect (explained further in chapter twenty-one). rippling away into other people, into other events and into other lives. and they choose to ripple, ripple, ripple, ripple and this is part of the Oneness. as if we are all water. together. when you drop, that drop of negativity it goes far and it reaches other people and they choose to ripple it out too or they can choose not to and they can choose to change that. this is up to them. they can choose this. but you are affecting others, as well as yourself and that ripple always comes back to you. so what we want you to see here: is when you choose love, you are rippling it out to yourself, to others; they are spreading it and nothing but love can come back to you - the source. you must choose yourself to be the source of this energy, if you want that. if you want love, you must choose love. you must choose to conduct love. you must choose to be Love. you must choose the ripple effect. you must choose The Light. and when you see that your actions affect others actions and they affect you ultimately (in how they come back to you). you will realize that all that you want to do is spread love and in so doing so receive love in return.

we are not saying this is easy at first. we are not saying that it is always going to happen right away. but if you choose this. if you make a conscious effort. conscious choice, to choose your thoughts, your actions, your beliefs, wisely and in love you will receive love back. and when you receive love back, you will be able to give more and more love and you will get more and more love back and it is nothing but a domino effect outside of the world. everyone will connect with this. everyone will move in this way and everything will happen out of love. we are not disjointed. we are all connected. and we want you to realize this. anyone can see this, anyone can see a bad day where they have fought with someone and their whole bad day turned into a domino effect of doing things in a negative way and  negative things coming back and biting them in the butt. and if it didn't happen that day, than it happened the next day. you cannot get away from something you did it's called karma. and it will connect you in a ripple effect. it may take a while, but it will come back to you always. if you choose to do things out of Love. Love conquers all.

so we want you to think on this: if you have been doing many, many things, that you are doing unconsciously or consciously negative and affecting others negatively that will come back to you. however if you choose right now, you choose this moment, to choose Love. consciously choose Love and choose that for other people and choose that for yourself and choose that for the world - you can remove the negativity coming back to you. you can remove it, because Love conquers all. Love conquers any negativity. so choose Love now and choose a future of Love. do not worry about negativity. do not worry about the past. do not worry about this moment, if you're choosing something that is not out of Love. choose Love. when you choose Love, you are choosing to conquer anything else and you will choose Love for the rest your life. it will come back to you again a hundred fold. you may not see it instantly, you may not see it tomorrow, you may not see it the next day. but I promise you this, you will feel better. and as you feel better, you will continue to choose Love and Love will come back to you.

so this is what we want to discuss today. yes, yes, yes, yes. this is good heather. yes, yes, continue on this. yes, yes, yes, you are channeling your higher-self. you are worried that you are just channeling yourself. you're channeling your higher-self and you are bringing forward much of the knowledge that you already know. much the knowledge that has already been passed through you through time and through generations and through different lives that you have lived. yes, yes, yes. now you understand why you act as a counselor and you understand what this ancient knowledge is that you possess. yes, yes, yes. you have tapped into this before and now you're choosing to tap into it again. this is good, this is good, this is good. this is what we want for the book. it is not completely just us talking through you, like we are right now. we want you to realize that you have a source inside yourself that is full of knowledge and that you're providing to everyone else. yes, yes, yes. you understand this now, don't you? *"yes i do."* and this is exactly what we want for this book. you are worried that we are not coming through you and that you're not receiving the right information. that you are just projecting your own thoughts and your own images into this book and that it will not be correct, will not be correct, will not be correct, and everyone will question it. because they will think it is channeled text, it is a channeled text, it is a channeled text. so why are things coming through just you? why is this most of your voice? because your voice is a higher-voice. the voice that is coming through you, is a higher voice and it is coming through you and is coming through at high-level and this is all energy that is coming through. and it is correct, correct, correct and you're doing this correctly. so do not worry, do not worry, do not worry. allow these things that you worry about to pass through you. allow them to go away. allow yourself to just relax. allow yourself to be you. the true you. the inner you. do not worry about this person. do not worry about this life. you have all the power that you need to move forward. to be who you need to be, to be the true you. allow this to come forward.

yes, yes, yes. we are working with you. we are working with your energy. we are allowing you to come forward. we want you to come forward. we want you to come forward, we want you to come forward. the real you. the real you. the real you. yes, yes, yes. the higher you. the Divine self. the Divine self. the Divine self. yes you are doing this, you are doing this, you are doing this. do not worry, do not worry, do not worry. yes you are wondering, "well i am taking different pieces of different information and from different subjects." this is good, this is good, this is good. we want you to take all this information and from different places that you have received it from and allow the world to see it, so that they can connect with this information. they can go out and they can read these books and they can connect with what you have connected with, as well. and choose the truth. choose the truth, choose the truth. project the truth. project the Love. from knowledge comes power. we are not talking about ego power. we are not talking about that at all. we are talking about Divine Will, we are talking about inner power, we are talking about the soul strength - we are talking about that. we are talking about the inner you, the good you. the Divine Will inside of you. we are talking about that part. so with that knowledge, good knowledge, true knowledge, truth, truth, truth you can empower this person. the real you. not to ego-self. the real-self, the inner-self. this person that is speaking most the time here. you are channeling a higher self, you're not channelling just yourself.

so we want to realize this. we want you trust this

information that is coming forward - trust it and bring it forward. yes, we'll come with you and we'll do edits at the very end. so do not worry, do not worry, do not worry. you're thinking, "oh my gosh, this book is going to go out exactly the way that I recorded it." and it will not. it will go out the way that it needs to go out, and we will go through it at a later time. but we want you to get used to channeling yourself, channeling yourself, channeling yourself, your higher self, your inner self. the knowledge that is within. you possess very much knowledge, because you in the past were a scholar and you are a scholar in this life. everyone is a scholar in their own right, in different ways. and so we want you to realize this, realize this, realize this. you have this ability, ability, ability inside of you. allow it to come forward. do not worry, do not worry, do not worry. yes very good allow yourself to relax.

(pause)

we want you to wrap up this chapter heather. we want you to end this here. we will allow you to move forward. allow yourself to continue with what you are doing right now. which is rocking back and forth. which is realigning yourself in the energy, the energy, the energy of the cosmos, cosmos. and we want you to do this. we want you to continue on this path and allow yourself to do this. but you may end your recording at this time. we are done for this evening and we thank you for your efforts and we are proud of what has happened this evening. you are moving in the direction that you need to. thank you, thank you, thank you, thank you. *love you guys.* we love you too. **amen.**

# Chapter Nine

# Clarification and Expansion

### Late Evening of February 27, 2013

yes, yes, heather. let us begin, let us begin, let us begin. we understand you are very tired. we can feel this in your energy system. we are working with you now to try to bring up your energy, so that you can bring through this book this evening. we understand, we understand, we understand. *what do you guys want to talk about this evening?* we would like to talk about love. let us continue with love. we know that you are getting tired of the topic. we know that you think that this topic is over, that it has been discussed enough, that we have gone through many chapters and that we have discussed this. we have already discussed this. we have already discussed this. but we have not discussed everything. we have talked about love and matrimony and we have talked about unconditional love. we have talked about many forms of love. but we still want to discuss Love. Love is very important. Love is the source

of all. Love is the undercurrent of everything that is going
on around you. Love is very important. Love is here for
everyone. Love is here for all. so we want this to be a very
big part of this chapter, very big part of this book, love,
love, love, love.

choosing love, as I said before, is very important,
very important. we want people to realize this. we want
people to realize this, this is very important, this is part of
life. this is what they need to do, this is what they need to
do, this is what they need to do. they need to allow
themselves to love, love, love, love and be loved. most
importantly to be loved. once you are loved, then you can
love others. when you are not loved completely, as you
know heather, as you know through your experience and
what has gone on in your history and in your past. loving
thyself is the most important and when you love thyself,
you can love anyone else. you can understand people, you
can love the earth, you can love everyone around you. and
you're still working on this, you are still working on this,
you are still working on this. yes, yes, yes, we understand
this. and everyone is probably working on this to some
degree. everyone is working through different things,
different feelings of guilt, different feelings of not being
good enough, different feelings that are of egoism. different
feelings of society saying, "you have to do things this way,
that way and you cannot be loved if you look like this or
you are that." this is wrong, this is wrong, this is wrong. we
want everyone to realize that they are loved. they are loved
and they are in love on a constant level. and they can
choose to align themselves with this or they can choose not
to. this is up to them, this is up to them, this is up to them.
they must decide whether or not they want to do this. just
as you have chosen that you do want to do this today. you
need to work on and everyday you need to work on
aligning yourself to this. aligning yourself to Love.

aligning, aligning, aligning. when you do this on a conscious level and when you start realizing that everything you do has to be in Love and through Love. you realize that this life can be nothing but Love. people of this world they say, "oh, all the horrible things. all these shootings, all this, that, the other thing. the economy. my sister. my mother. my brother. my friend. my, this sworn enemy, this person, that person." and they look at all the negatives in life rather than looking at the positives. and we want them to look at the positives. we want them to look at the positives, look at the positives, look at the positives, look at the positives and look at love. look at everything through love. realize that if everyone that you looked at was an animal. yes, yes, yes. you're referring to what holly has seen and what she has told you. yes, go ahead and share this example with them: *(this example was shared in the previous chapter. love thy neighbor as thyself).*

*okay. so, the example that i want to share is: that my sister while we were doing some energy healing for me to get to this place, to be able to bring through this book. we had a discussion basically about uhmmm...a practice that you do in i am the word. which is to visualize yourself in a room with people and you visualize them thinking that they are better than you and holding all the knowledge and how you would feel in that situation. would you go around asking a bunch of questions? trying to get the knowledge or would you feel insecure? how would you feel? and then imagine yourself as if you had all the knowledge in the world and everyone is coming to you. how would you feel? would you feel like, "why are you coming to me? I don't have any more knowledge than anyone else." would you feel superior to everyone else and more authoritative and ego-centered?*

*then the next example is to imagine yourself as equally knowledgeable as everyone else in the room and that you're basically trying to come from a place of to love. compassion and understanding. so my sister, always being into animals and animal totems for different people. instead of visualizing people as they were, she visualizes them is their animal totem. and seeing them for who they are as an animal and finding love for them. obviously all animals have good and bad qualities to them. even your most favorite dog has probably chewed up a sock or two and you haven't loved it for doing that, at that moment. but you loved it on a deeper level than its' actions.*

*so this is the concept of unconditional love. this feeling that you can look at people and look at them as if they are their animal totem or your favorite dog or whatever it is that you feel unconditional love for and allow their little mistakes, allow their ways of doing things to not hurt you, affect you and come into your energy system. but instead to only feel love, true love. is very important. yes, that is the example that that i wanted to share with you. so lets see what else they want to say.*

yes, this is very good heather. yes, we are glad that you shared this example with everyone and we are glad that you were able to get that through. yes, so we want people to be able to understand this - to understand that to look at everyone in love, is to look at them as if they are in unconditional love. that although they may do wrong or they may do things that you may not like, (in your discernment of things) they are still loved. they are still unconditionally loved, no matter, no matter what they do. you look at them as a child, you look at them as your child and as they are learning things just as you are learning, you learn to forgive. and this is also a way to look back at anything that you think you have done and anything that you have done in your past and you think you cannot forgive yourself for. look at things in the past as you have been learning them as a child would learn and look at them and laugh at them - allow them to be released. allow them to be released in love and say thank you for these experiences and these things that have taught you and have brought you to where you are today. if you do not like the state you are in today. you can change it. you choose to change. you choose your future. you choose the now. so choose, choose, choose Love. when you choose Love, you choose a beautiful bright future for yourself. and this is what we want you to do. this is what we want you to do: we want you to continue on with this. yes, yes, continue heather, continue. continue. *yes. basically continue to grab onto love. allow yourself to hold it. allow yourself to embrace it and continue through this. when you choose Love you are choosing a beautiful bright future. you are choosing this moment.* discuss, discuss, discuss. discuss what you thought of today while you were at work. discuss, discuss, discuss.

*okay i have another example of feeling this: in realizing the energy source around me. while, i was sitting working at my parents hot tub store and often times i have hours there to just think and ponder. which is great for me to realize things. i noticed a kind of a visual shift, i guess, between everything as far as the walls and everything around me. just to get into the state of solidarity. in love and peace. you can really see that everything is vibrating at a level around you. and so everything you see. in a way. is a creation of what you want to see.* **you are projecting it into your visual consciousness and therefore it is existing. and you can change anything around you. you can change it, you can change, you can change it.**

*so basically i'm just coming into this realization that everything around me is a choice. everything that i see is a choice. everything is an energy level and can change. nothing is permanent like we think it is. which I thought was a very interesting concept because we visualize everything as solid.*

*the thing is i guess, it's easier for me to sit here and say, "yes, yes, i* can see all these things and i can tell you what they are." but until you experience them. until you are ready to experience them. until you choose to experience these things and see these things. you are not really going to understand what's going on here. so that's why there is a patience level and a desire to have this information that's very important. if you desire it. if you want it. if you love it. if you're interested, excited about it, then of course it will come to you. you will be able to feel these experiences and give things to other people as well as yourself.

so that's another thing i wanted to say, i guess, is that i think it's very easy for someone like myself and other people that are going through channeling and are experiencing these things to write a book about them. but the reader, if they have not chosen to do some of these things (channeling, shamanic journeying, etc.), they don't quite understand or grasp the concept. it's just like when you're a child and you're trying to learn math or you are trying to read and the person teaching you has already gotten to this certain level of knowledge, they already understand it. so, in a way, it's like telling the child, "this is how you do it. okay this is how you do it. this is how you work through it. this is how you get there." to the teacher it is easy. they have already accomplished it and to the child they are frustrated because they're not quite understanding or grasping the material. so, i guess, this is where the level of love comes in. the love and patience, that you know that you are going to connect on an energy level and you are going to bring that person up to the level that they need to be at. this is what i want, this is what i want, this is what i want. i want to bring people up to a higher level. i want to bring people to this because they can do it. if i can do this in six months so can anyone else. if i can do it, than anyone else can do it. and this is what i told myself when i was watching other channelers and mediums or i was getting a psychic reading done by someone else. i was saying, "well if this person can do it, so can i." and that's a pretty bold statement coming from this feeling, pressed in usually by society, that someone has to be gifted with these experiences. they have to be given this blessing from God and this talent from God, in order to be able to do these things. not everyone can do them. and so why can i? so there are mental blocks you have to go through and you have to a breakthrough just like when you're trying to learn math or you are trying to learn a subject. you have to go through all these mental blocks. and when you go through them and you come out the other side. you are like, "oh wow. i understand now. i get it, i get it, i get it."

so i want this book to be a realization of how it is, to really go through these experiences and trying to connect with your guide(s). try to actually bring these teachings into your daily life, because trust me when i say this. it does not mean that on a daily basis, i am so great at doing these things [the lessons they teach]. i am learning them. i am doing them. but when you connect with your teachers, when you connect with your spirit guides, they give you a frequency, which is hard to explain, they give you a frequency of, "you've got it, your getting it, yeah, yeah you've got it." just like a teacher or a coach is trying to get you to learn something. even though you may be frustrated trying to get to that point, trying to get to this sort of level that you need to be at, that you know you can obtain. so just realize that even though when you're going through this process you may be feeling like, "i'm never going to get there." and you may be feeling frustrated and that you don't have a full grasp of all the information. you have someone from the other side cheering you on and helping you through the whole entire thing. so this isn't just the process of you doing it on your own, as you feel sometimes. often times you just feel like, "oh man, i'm doing this on my own and no one is helping me and i'm not getting the information right." and you start second guessing yourself and you will get it. and it's all faith and it's all patience and it's timing and it's being excited and thirsty for the knowledge and the experience. and then you will receive what you need to receive to make it happen. so that is something i definitely wanted to share with you. let's see…let me get back to them. i think they might want to add some other things into this evening.

yes, this is very good heather. yes, we wanted you to share this experience, to get this off of your chest. because you wanted to share this, you have wanted to get this into the book for a very long time. and we know that you think that certain things are out of place and yes they are, they are, they are. but everything will be coming in together, and everything will work. and then when it is all in together, then we will go through it and we'll make it fit the way that we wanted it to fit; the way that it needs to be fit. do not worry, do not worry, do not worry. everything will work out, everything will work, everything will fit together, and everything will be joined. just as you were saying: you are the student and we are the teachers. and we are coming through you and we're trying to get you to the level that you need to get to. you think you need to do things a certain way, but you do not. you can do things in a different ways and we will get you there, we'll get you there, we'll get you there. so we would like you to stop worrying so much about what you feel needs to happen and the way it needs to happen and to stop holding on and stop trying to control the process. stop trying to do that. allow it to come, allow it to come, allow it to come. let it just be free-form, free-form, free-form. just like when you used to free write in college, when you used to do that. just allow this to come through you. all the information will work together. the reader will receive the information. you think it's going to be discombobulated, disjointed. and the reader is not going to understand what's going on here and they are just going to think, "well this information is not coming together for me, so i can't understand it, so therefore i cannot connect." this is not true, this is not true, this is not true. everyone will understand this information. they will get it, they will get it, they will get it. we will write it in a way that people will understand, understand, understand.

so do not worry about this. you are concerned that the way this is coming through is very hodgepodge, is all over the place and we agree some of it is. but that's okay, because these are topics that you choose on a daily basis and we are saying yes, you choose, you choose, you choose. not just us. we want you to feel that way and we want the reader to feel that way. this information coming through are things that you need to go through. the knowledge that you need to know and this will also be knowledge that other people need to know. so we want you to realize this is not just you. not just you, not just you and it is not just us, not just us, not just us. it is a relationship, like we said before. it is a relationship, it is a relationship, it is a relationship. we are working together, together, together.

so yes, allow yourself to continue on with this information. this is okay, this is okay, this is okay. yes, you are thinking (and we will repeat this again) that we are processing just this information or that you are just processing this information and it is coming through and it is wrong, it is wrong, it is wrong. and it's not wrong - it is right, it is right, it is right. we will go through at the very end. we'll make changes, we'll delete things if we need to delete things. but most likely they will not need to be deleted. trust us, trust us, trust us. anything that you see as an error will not be errors to others. and it will show that there are things that people need to know that, need to know, need to know, need to know. maybe you do not need to know them, but other people will need to know them. they will need to realize that things come through and sometimes they are discombobulated. sometimes they don't come through the exact way they want it to come through and that is okay, that is okay, that is okay. everything will come through and everything will work out.

so it does not matter, it does not need to happen the way they need it to happen. we need people to allow us to come in, come in, come in. allow the reigns to go away. you are seeing yourself basically riding a horse, allow them [the reigns] to release, release, release. we are the horse, we will take you to the place that you need to be taken to. allow yourself to just enjoy the ride. look around and enjoy the things that are going on and enjoy the frequency of the horse moving, moving, moving. as you need to get to the place that you need to go to. so yes, yes, yes, this is very important. we want people to just realize that they need to relax, relax, relax, relax. they live in a society were everything is about go, go, go, go, go, go, go. and it does not need to be about that. it needs to be about them, it needs to be about the self, it needs to be about relaxation. relaxation will give time for the self to think and re-evaluate and re-align to its' higher-self.

when you are in these relaxed meditative states, you can re-align to were you need to go and when you get to that place. you do not need to think as much. you do not need to try to push as much. you do not need to try and get this and this and this and this done, right now, right now, this second, this second. in order for this person or that person or the other person to be happy. it is about you and it is about relaxing. and once you realize that you are happy and that when you are happy others are happy. so therefore, what you do is say, okay, it is okay, it is okay, it is okay. you stop trying to do all these things, all these things, all these things, to make others happy. and you start doing the things that you need to do, you need to do, you need to do, to be happy.

so we want people to realize that they are in this place where they are often times trying to make others happy and by doing so they're not making themselves happy. and when they are not making themselves happy, other people can see this. can see this, can see this. can feel this, feel this, feel this, even more and that is even more important. when they feel this, then they are not happy and they are coming back and they are not happy with you and then you continue to not be happy because they are not happy and it is a cyclical effect and it continues, it continues, it continues. like the dominoes that we were talking about. like the the drop and the waves that we were talking about - *the ripple effect*. yes, yes, this is right heather.

so yes, we want people to realize this. so making yourself, yourself, happy, is number one. and this is coming from a society where if you're thinking about yourself. then you're being egotistical. well we are talking differently about the ego, we're talking about the inner good. the inner self, the higher self, the person inside, the soul self: that needs nourishment, that needs your time, that needs to feel loved and realize that you are loved. there is a source inside of you that is so wanting to come out. in everyone, and it wants to come out and it wants share itself with everyone else. and connect with everyone else on their soul selves, and soul state.

we want people to realize this, they can, they can, they can, they can do this. so when they do this, their lives will change in ways that they will see out-picturings change. not everything will be, "i must get this done for everyone else." it will be, "i must get this done, if i choose to get this done, and it should be done for myself." it'll be different. people will think differently. behave differently, act towards others differently and in return the same will be done for them. people will not ask others to do things they know the other will not need or want to do. because they will feel their energy. often times people that are asking you to do things for them, it's because they need to do things for themselves. so this is where we are saying tough love comes in. i'm sure you've heard this from your parents or from your mother who said, "well that's just tough. tough love." and we are saying this is good, this is good, this is good. you can only give, you can only do so much for so many people without doing something for yourself. others are not here just to give to you and serve you and do what you want to do and what you want them to have done for you. people are eager to please and they will do the things that need to be done for you. but it will be out of love. they will love you and do it for themselves; to feel more love, more connection with your love and spread this love, connected love, to other people. and we are trying to express how this is different. when you're asking others to do things for you, there is a separateness there, often times. you're acting as if they owe you something. no one owes you anything. you owe yourself something and when you give yourself what you need. others can give you what you need as well, as long as, it's coming from a place of love.

this is what we're saying love, love, love, love, love. you thought this chapter was over, heather. now you see, you see, you see. there's so much information, so much that is tied into Love: this earth is Love, the plants around you are Love, the air is Love, the molecules are Love, the energy is Love - everything is Love. everything is Love. you would not be here today without Love, love, love, love. so we want you to realize this. we want the world to realize this and embrace this. embrace Love, true Love, and allow it to flow from that. and we are not saying this is gonna be easy at first. we are not going to say that you are not going to have to get rid of some of these things. you're seeing dirty water, or whatever it is, heather. yes, the dirty particles because we're filling you with clean water and as we fill you with clean water the things that are particles that have been settled, that have been down there, are going to float up. and they're going to percolate in your system. and you're going to have to deal with them and get rid of them. and allow them to wash away from you. and as they wash away from you and you bath yourself in clean water every day, clean loving water. this is what will stick, this is what will stay and you will be full. so we are not saying that you go to war and you battle all these things inside you. you will see them, they will come up, you will recognize them for what they are and you will decide to choose Love over them.

*often times*, this is what heather wants to speak of right now. *i will drive and as i am driving, i get very upset with other people. i get competitive and i want to pass them. make sure that i am in front of them. and this is not from a state of love, this is from a state of ego. i don't want them to pass me. it is also from a state of fear, that all the sudden i'm not going to be number one if i'm not up in front. so i'm learning, that the state that this puts me in is not a good one. it is not good, it overcomes my body. it overcomes me and it's not what i want to be, and it's not the person i want to be. it's not spreading love and i realize this. if i choose to act upon this, i am choosing to give this to myself and allow it to be given to other people and continue on and on. and this is the hardest thing that i am dealing with on a daily basis, is trying not to allow myself to get into an anger state, a competitive state, a separateness state from my brother in the car next to me, or my sister in the car next to me. who is driving maybe not the way that i want them to drive. who i get competitive with, because i want to make sure that i'm in front, so that i don't feel like the back of the pack or whatever. because i'm type a personality and i'm a person that likes to be in the front, i'm a leader and this is how i am, this is my personality. but i need to learn that sometimes a great leader needs to be led. and to allow myself, in order to feel peace, not to feel his competitive nature.*

*and so this is what they're talking about with love, love, love, love, love. choosing love and choosing not to go to battle with all these little pieces of things that are coming up and rather instead of going to battle with them just allow it to slip away. coming into a peace state. come to this state of relaxation. realize that the person next to you driving is your brother, your sister, a friend, whoever you want to think of it as. and then by behaving poorly you are maybe hurting them and in return you are hurting yourself. this is what i mean, allow yourself to relax away from this, to calm down. so whatever you have problems with, whatever rises those things up. whatever you notice are your little specks of debris, that are slowly being cleansed out of your system. allow them to come. embrace them. learn from them. do not go to war with them. by going to war with them you are only giving them more energy and where the energy goes the energy stays. so do not give them more energy. allow them to move through you. move out of your system. and when you do this, you are allowing purity. you're allowing the pure self, the higher self to come in. and i'm not saying this is going to happen overnight. it takes time. it takes work. it takes effort. so this is what I'm saying and* this is what we are saying. yes, this is what we're saying yes, yes, yes, continue with this.

we are all One. we are all connected and when you choose Love, you choose One. you choose it and you choose not to be separate and this is what we want, this is what we want, this is what we want. we are coming back to this every single time. and we are coming back to this, we are coming back to this, we are coming back to this - choice. choice, choice, choice. choose Love. when you choose Love, you choose Oneness. when you choose Oneness, you're choosing Love and you're choosing yourself. you are choosing your higher self and you're choosing your brothers, your sisters and you're choosing a state of peace.

we're in this society where we feel like we must succeed, must succeed, must succeed, must succeed. what does success mean? well that is different for every person, isn't it? *often times it is social. often times it is family related. often times it is some sort of pressure that they have put on themselves. what success truly is, is to feel happy. when will you feel happy? when you have all these things that you want? then will you feel happy? let me tell you what happiness is: happiness is feeling at peace and at One with thyself. and when one feels One with thyself, they feel in Love with the self. so peace, Love and Oneness all go together. and when you realize it, when you come to a state of peace with everything around you and with where you are at. this term success, defined by becoming a ceo, or a movie star or the next great big thing. does not seem as important. that peace state, that love state, that is the state that everyone needs to be at.* **and they will be taking care of that, everyone will be taken care of. and no one will need to worry about this thing called money. monetary, monetary, monetary. money, money, money, money. no one will need to worry about this.** everyone will do the things they want to do for themselves and they will be doing them for the One, for the consciousness, for it is superior consciousness that is coming.

and this is what we want to say: this is coming, this is coming, this is coming. whether you choose to be on the tidal wave, as heather was talking about, or seeing last night her dream. whether you choose to be out on the tidal wave or stand on the beach, you will be swept up in this. you will not be allowed to think that there is not such a thing as One consciousness and this is not coming from a state of fear. we are not trying to invoke fear here. we're not trying to tell you that something is going to happen that is going to be scary. we're not trying to come from state of control. we are just telling you what is. what is. what is. and what will be soon in your realm. you can no longer live in the paradigm that you live on a flat earth, because you do not. you can no longer live in the paradigm that you [the earth] are the center of the universe, because you are not. so we want you to realize this: this paradigm shift is coming. it will come. and it is on its way. so you can choose to ride the tidal wave and you can choose to be part of the adventure, the excitement that is coming. or you can choose to be swept up in it and you will be swept up in it and you will allow it to come into your system at some point or another. this is up to you, this is up to you, this is up to you, this is up to you. choose, choose, choose where you would like to be in this paradigm shift. choose, choose, choose. heather has something that she wants to say:

*well, it was just about fear basically. the quote i heard yesterday, in a song by Awolnation, "do not let fear decide your fate."* **and this is true, this is true, this is true. you have to allow this to shift. you have to allow yourself to look at these fears, look at them for what they are and see them as silly nonsense of the out-picturing of what you think could happen. and this is not true. this is not true. this is not true.**

you will not have anything to worry about with this change, with this shift. and so we want you to realize and start to analyze your fears and see where they're coming from. see how they did not have anything, any real meaning to you. allow your garden to be removed from these weeds. allow yourself to grow, allow yourself to grow, allow yourself to grow. remove these weeds, remove them, remove them, remove them. fear has no state any longer. fear has no reason. fear has no purpose. fear is no more. choose this, choose this, choose this. so yes we want you to think of yourself as a garden and every single time you think of something that you are in fear of. we want you to analyze it, look at it, and see what it is and understand it for what it is. and then we want you to remove this from your garden as if it is a weed. and we are showing this picture to heather right now. she is a bunch of flowers in the garden and as she slowly removes these weeds, she is allowed to move further up in her psych and in her ability to reach the sun and to reach further growth. so this is what we want you to do, we want you to do, we want you to do. take home this practice with you.

yes, heather we are done for this evening. we realize that you're tired. yes, yes, yes, yes. we've gotten much done, much done, much done. we have done well, we've done well. we've done well. yes, yes, yes. you may take a break. come back to us in the morning. *sounds good, sounds good*. we love you. *love you too*. and we thank you for your work today and we appreciate all that you have done and we are very excited for this book. and we want you to continue to be excited about it as well. allow your energy to move into this excitement state, every single morning before you come in here, and every single evening allow yourself to get excited about the information that is coming to you. because you are learning, learning, learning every single time. and this is what the reader is doing as well. and we want this energy to come through, come through, come through. *thank you and goodnight*.

# Chapter Ten

## My Q&A

we are ready to begin heather. it is time, it is time, it is time. *what do you guys want to discuss today?* we want to discuss some of the things that you have discovered. *will this be added into the book?* yes, yes it will. we will decide where it will be added later. do not worry, do not worry, do not worry. this is free form, free form, free form. this whole book is that way. you think that it is a specific order and that things have to come certain ways. but they do not, they do not, they do not. everything will be put into this book the proper way. everything will be put in the way that it needs to be done. we are not saying that we're doing this right now, that we're doing it chronologically, things may be put in different places. but we must discuss, must discuss, must discuss. *okay sounds good.* so go ahead, continue with what you are thinking and some of your

notes you have written down. go ahead and allow yourself
to talk about these things and we'll come to you and your
higher-self will come through you and we will talk about
them in a way that will be reached on an energy level.
mmm...k. sounds good.

okay. so some of the things i discovered last night, which was great,
from my mom. while i was waiting for my daughter to come home,
we decided to watch a youtube video on this guy. his name is michael
newton and he is a hypnotherapist. prior to his discovery of a past-
life experiences during one of his normal a session with a
gentleman, newton proclaimed himself to be an atheist. his beliefs
changed after several more of the encounters and the patients ability
to be detailed about their experiences and their accuracy in their
past lives. so, now, after several years in this profession he has
changed from his traditional work of classic hypnotherapy to
become a past-lives hypnotherapist. he works on helping people
through any remaining feelings from a past-lives that they feel here
and help them move forward.

one of the things i was struggling with during this process
was the thought of being One with everyone, loving thy neighbor.
especially in the case of murders, rapist. etc. i didn't have all of the
information to bring forward or feel that the subject was completed.
this is what your guides will do sometimes. they will give you
information in different ways, rather than through them. this is
done for many reasons. in this case, i believe, it was so that the
information would be accessible to others. anyways, during the
youtube video newton discusses this process in the afterlife with
people we consider to have done "great evil." he explains that from
his experience doing hypnotherapy with these individuals, he finds
nothing but a loving spirit world. he says, people that have done
these acts, often times gladly choose to go back as the victim. to
learn their lesson from the other point of view.

which i found very interesting when you think of the, "eye for
an eye" concept we hold ourselves to, here in the u.s. - justice will be

served. the spirit world takes care of this on its' own. if you are looking at it from a spiritual world, everything will be justified and spirit realm takes great compassion on these people that have done these acts of evil. these people choose to come back as a victim and really choose to learn from this experience from the others perspective. so this is very interesting, when you really begin to think about it. **this life is about learning, learning, learning.** this life is not about just this singular life and that we don't go on learning. we have had many, many past lives and many future lives to go through and we are all at different stages as far as our soul growth.

so that was definitely one of the things i struggled with and it was discussed earlier in the book when i was channeling. i was bringing it through the best way that i could, which was that everyone comes from love. i mean i definitely struggle with the thought of being One with the rapist or the murderer because that is something i do not choose. but just because you have not chosen it, does not mean that you are not One with them. and One on this path of learning and One on this path of love. One on this path of the end destination that will teach you more and more and more. we have no reason to judge others. in all reality we do not. the beings of Light that have chosen to snuff out The Light of others will come back and they will learn their lesson - justice will be served. now this is hard to say and probably hard to swallow for the people that have had their loved ones taken away from them. but as newton says, they [the victims] have chosen this. they have chosen this life. they have chosen this experience to learn from for their soul growth. everything that was here. everything that has happened in our lives, we have chosen that. we have chosen it whether it is here now, to choose as a choice day-by-day. or whether we have chosen to be re-incarnated with the knowledge of what this life will bring and what lessons it will teach us. we realize that, wow, we have several lives and there are different planes and different places to learn these lessons that we need to learn. and basically we can do no wrong. especially if we are coming from a state of love. if you are coming *from a state of love, then there is no ability for this wrong. so there is no reason to judge another or to fear.*

*when you release this grid of fear and you come from a place of love. whatever you do, no matter what it is, you can do no wrong. so there is no reason to fear, there is no reason to fear death or to fear these people that have done these 'wrongs.' because in reality they are learning their lessons that they need to learn here and they will come back and they will learn them again, and the next time from the other persons side. i want to wrap up with this thought of being One and the realization now that with this information we can forgive and become whole.*

*"do not be so quick to judge the victim," - rhonda byrne, the power. we do not know what may have transpired in a previous lifetime that they are now a victim.*

(pause)

yes we are here heather. we are ready to begin. we are ready to speak. we are ready, we are ready, we are ready. yes, yes. the topic that you brought up yes, yes, this is very good. yes, you were struggling with this concept and yes we did bring you this youtube video for you through your sister and mother. and this is the way this world works. we try to bring in messages whether you are in contact with us or not. we want people to realize, we are always trying to bring the messages to them. messages, messages, messages, from the other world. from the other world, as they see it. but we are all here. we are One. we are all part of this world. just because there is a veil and you cannot see us necessarily does not mean that we do not exist here.

if you look at children, if you're looking at your child or any other child and watch them, you watch them play, you hear. for example, heather, you have child and you

hear her playing in her crib and you hear her talking to
other people and you hear her laughing with other people.
you know, you know, you know. she is talking with her
guides, she is talking with people from the spirit world. she
is not alone. so you are not alone. this world is not full of
lonely people roaming around trying to find themselves
and trying to learn their lessons without any guidance. you
can choose this path. you can choose it, you can choose it,
you can choose it. and many of you have, because you
believe you have no other options. you believe that you are
stuck here on this planet, isolated, by yourself and you are
alone and learning these lessons with other people around
you watching, staring, judging. but this is wrong, this is
wrong, this is wrong. this world is full of Love. this world
is full of Oneness. everyone is your brother, your sister.
often times if you ask people for help, they will help you
and they will allow you into their Love system and
everyone is part of the One. they are trying to move
forward, they are trying to move forward in their life and
they are trying to move to the next stage. and they are
trying to learn lessons that they are here to learn. and then
you have a spirit realm, you have all your spirit guides
here, waiting, ready to help you. so when you choose this,
you choose this, you choose this. for us to come here and
for us to help you, we can do so. we will do so. and we are
here. so this is something of choice. again we want to
discuss this: choice, choice, choice.

you are not alone. you're never alone, as you suspect
and you think. you are full of Love. you are full of God's
love. you're here, you're here, you're here - to be filled with
Love. to be filled with love and to fill others with love and
to learn, learn, learn, learn. and we are here to help you.
you are not isolated. you're not alone, you are not alone,
you are not alone. we are here, we are here, we are
physically here and an energy source at all times for you.

just as everything else is here in an energy source. yes, you can see this. you can knock on wood. you can do whatever you need to do. you can touch the ground, you can touch everything around you and so therefore you feel that it is concrete. but it is not concrete. if anyone has done any of their research, as far as quantum physics and things of that nature and energy levels. everything is moving at an energy level. the density is what allows you to touch it and this is what allows you to believe that it is real it is physical. it is here. it is here. it is right now. so we want you to realize this: this, all of this, is movable. it is tangible and intangible, as we are. so we can come into your system anytime. so heather we want you discuss. yes, yes, we see what you trying to say. yes go ahead and discuss what you were thinking of earlier what you have written down in your notes about meeting your guides and things of that nature.

*okay one of the things that i wanted to discuss early that i have been writing down a bunch of notes and things that pop into my mind. and i know they don't just pop in there, it is basically they're [my guides] feeding me information and allowing me to go through this information and think of things i want to say out loud, so that they get written in this book and they get added in there.*

*so anyways one of the things I wanted to bring up was an example of something. often times when people are trying to figure out how to meet their guides or what their guides will feel like or how this will all go. if they will be upset that they haven't been talking to their guides...or whether their guides will be there or not. this is my example of the thought that they have brought to me: so you have a great friend. a friend that you have known for a really long time, that you are really good friends with. one of those people you click with. you just know who they are. you know all about them and you just have an energy frequency and you connect with them. i am sure that you have had at least one of these people: friend, relative, whomever it may be. and then often times what happens with friends you grow up and things happen, people move on, they have children, they move, they go to a different state, they go to a different country. and you slowly become busy with all the things that you think that you need to be doing here on this earth. and you loose touch, you loose contact. and then usually 10 - 15 - 20 years down the road, you get back in touch with them, spontaneously, or they do with you. you meet up and once again you instantly connect again. this connection, this frequency, there is lots of laughter, lots of love is always happening. and this has always been there. just because you have separated and moved on and been focused and busy with other things. does not mean that that hasn't always been there for you or the other person to reach out and have a connection.*

*this is the same with the spirit guides. so, if you ask your parents they will admit to you in truth, that you used to talk with guides and you used to have conversations in your bed and you used to say you saw people. then as you grow older in society, it's not status quo to be speaking to these people and doing these things. then all the sudden you're not allowed to talk to them and you're separated from them. so you separate and you move on and they are still there. they are helping other people and they are watching over you and delivering messages as best they can. and trying to get other people to deliver their messages to you for them. and then one day you decide hey, "i am going to reach out, i am going to connect with these people." or you go through an event that causes this connection to occur, such as a near death experience. and you wonder if that person is still going to like you and know you after all these years just like your old friend. and as you instantly connect you once again know them for who they are.* **you know them, you know them, you know them. you have lots of laughter and fun and you realize that you are never alone. you are never alone, you are never going through this experience alone. they are always their. and you were separating from them because of choice, choice, choice. choosing, choosing, choosing. and maybe it**

**wasn't time for you to re-connect. maybe you needed to learn the lessons that you needed to learn before you could reconnect with them.** *and everyone has different times in different frequencies for this. some people will not connect with them in this lifetime.* **they will choose not to, choose not to, choose not to. and that is fine, that is fine, that is fine. they can move onto the next life and they will do whatever they need to do in the next life. so there's no doing any wrong. if you come from a place of love. if you come from place of learning you need to do for you and your connecting with you guides if you feel that you need to do this for yourself.**

*which in my case I did and I knew that I needed to and I knew that I wanted to. and I was ready for this experience. then you will and they are always there and they always love you and there is lots of laughter. lots of love. yes just like any relationship with anyone, there is some frustration because you ask them, "why have you left me alone?" and it's because you chose it. so you come back to the place of a choice and you realize everything you've chosen. every reason that all of these things have happened to you. that are positive or negative, however you view them, which is again your choice - you've chosen. so when you're reaching out to your guides, do not be afraid. do not worry, "oh they are going to judge me. oh i haven't connected with them. oh they have probably been waiting around for me forever."* **no, no, no, no, they're here waiting for you in love and they will speak to you whenever you're ready and this is up to you, this is to you, this is up to you.**

*so this is one of the things that i want to discuss with you today and that is one of the topics that I think needs to be brought about. because all the books that I have read, which they have been great - great books and I will definitely talk about them in my book because I think that they are great. yes they want me to discuss this. one of my things, one of my passions is to network with other people. i'm all about relationships in this lifetime - i believe. and it is about connecting with people and sharing all their information with everyone else. because we're all One, all One, all One. and so I'm not worried about the profits of this book going out the window because someone else reads another book. I am here to help help help you - the reader. get to whatever state it is that you want to be at. and I have some really great books that can bring you to wherever you need to go. and they are great kickoff points to channeling. and some of these books might not work for you. and some of them may and I'm just here to bring forward the information that has been given to me. and this is what I want, this is what I want, this is what I want* and this what we want, what we want, what we want. yes we want people to realize that everyone can share with everyone else. this is not a business world. everyone thinks that this is business, business, business, business and i must protect myself, must protect myself, must protect myself. this is a place of fear, fear, fear, and we don't want people to do this anymore. we want people to realize they can network, they can exchange information. they can become a team, everyone is teaming. everyone is working together, working together, working together. yes yes yes this is relationship, relationship building. yes heather this is what you want, you are here to do, this is what you are here to do, this is what you are here to do and this book will be part of that. yes yes yes yes. so bring this forward. bring this forward, bring this forward.

*okay. okay, uhmmm...let me see if there was anything else I wanted to talk to you about or whether they have anything. okay yes, one of the things that we just touched on basically, that i wanted to talk about.* yes yes yes go ahead continue heather. yes allow yourself to look at these things. you will not break the connection with us as you think you will. *one of the things that we keep striving for while we are here on this earth and one of the things that I have striven for is success. progression, moving* forward, moving forward, moving forward and yes this is part of the soul world. moving forward into your next soul path. so that is part of the reason why we get this feeling in this life. part of why we feel that we need to move forward constantly. because it is what we want upon this earth and that is what I am trying to explain here. yes. that is part of the reason sometimes why we feel, we get in a rut, we get stuck with things. and we need to make changes to move on and move forward. it is because we are trying to learn lessons in our lives and we do not want to be stagnate and we want to move forward. but sometimes we do not know how to do this. i mean i was at a block, when i was going on vacation to sedona. i had separated from my ex-fiance. i was now moving into a world of single-hood. i was moving into a different life, that i hadn't planned on. and i was choosing this, to be honest. i was choosing to move forward and choosing to move into this different world. but of course it comes with a feeling of being lost and directionless. i just kept feeling this motion to move forward, move forward, move forward. go on this vacation to sedona and this is where everything happened. this is where it all spun into what i am doing right now.

so you will be given direction if you ask for it. this is what people need to learn to do. ask for the things that you want. and the things that you are meant to have you will receive answers for. so you must understand this. you may think that your path is this and it must go this way, and this is how it must go. but this is not true. allow things to come, to come to you, allow things to flow through you, allow yourself to be engaged with the things that you are meant to do. and allow yourself to love every single moment of it. do not be reaching so forward into the future that you cannot enjoy today. allow yourself to be connected with today. this is what you need to do. do not be over-reaching into tomorrow. do not allow the past to take up too much time today. allow yourself to focus on the here, the now, and everything else will work out. so allow yourself to not worry so much about progression and moving forward. just allow yourself to be here and happy with what is going on. this is one of the hardest things that we have a time with, or at *least that I had a time with. this is part of what I was saying earlier, is that you are connected with the spirit realm. i mean ask yourself this question here right now, "can you imagine yourself ever not existing?" I definitely can't. just because i came from a womb. doesn't mean that I didn't come from somewhere before that. how could i not exist before that? and then in this way, if you can't imagine yourself never existing, then you can't imagine yourself not existing when you die and you move on. you will always move on. there will always be a cyclical effect. you will move, you will move, you will move, you will be teaching or you will be taught. it depends on what you are doing in your life and what you are here to do. so that is one thing that I wanted to bring up today.*

*these other things, one of these things that i was noticing as i was going through this process. (what i am talking about here is when i moved out from living with my ex and back in with my parents). is i think what happened, is one night i was channeling. i was channeling and thinking about all the truth in words. truth in these little things, in these little proverbs, that have been passed down from different generations and cultures over time. how these little truths are really big truths, they have infinite power and they are really left here by us, our ancestors, to help us move through. and they are like little gems of information and knowledge, to help us move through into our lives. and really allow ourselves to become part of One. to allow us to move through any of these feelings that we have as being an egoist body or creature. and allow us to move through those blockages and become centered on our path. which is to become One and either to teach or to be taught* the knowledge, the knowledge, the knowledge. becoming One. becoming One. yes yes yes this is good heather continue continue continue. you think that you are not bringing this forward but you are, you are, you are.

(long discussion with my guides on other topics i wanted to bring forward. They chose to postpone this discussion for another time.)

we think that the work you have done here today is very good. yes yes yes you have brought forward all the information that we want you to bring forward today. this is good, this is good, this is good. we want the other things to sit with you for a little while. we may end up channeling them later tonight or maybe a different day. but we want those things to sit with you a little while, re-evaluate the way you want them to be said. and the energy level that you want them to come forward. you do not want to be scolding people or teaching them saying, "you do this and you do that." we want you to bring them from a place of love. we want you to have love love love love. just as other people reading this book will love this book for what it is and allow it into their system. and this is what we want, this is what we want, this is what we want. this is very important, important, important. it is not so much the words written on the page as it is the energy and frequency behind them that we feel is very important. so we want you to realize this, realize this, realize this. so allow yourself to take a break. allow yourself to re-evaluate the information that you want to bring forward in this next chapter. we thank you very much for your time heather, you have done a great job and we are going to allow you to move on today and think of these things in the past. we thank you so much for your time. love you very much. *you too. amen. name of the Father, Son, Holy Spirit. amen.*

# Chapter Eleven

# The Influence

## Notes Before Channeling Session

we are constantly evaluating the things we have in our lives in comparison to others. many of us are trying to live up the jonses and therefore create from lack in our own lives. instead we should be looking at all that we have and be grateful for these things. the simplest things such as clean air to breath, running water, a car, family, etc. then we will be creating from abundance of how much we already have. also when choosing the things we want in our lives we will not choose them because others have them, therefore we must. we should choose them because we truly desire and love them. this life in not about evaluating against others, it is about evaluating internally our true desires. in a society where we are concerned with fitting in, if we do not have such and such or look such and such way, this concept can be hard to implement in your daily life. but when you look through history, the people that made their mark didn't try to be like everyone else. they were themselves and they "pushed the envelope" with their own imagination and *determination to be their true selves.*

*as a culture we take topics and we like to separate them for better understanding. however whatever topic, no matter how small you look at it, it is combined with any other topics. it all flows together, just as we all flow together. we like to take people and separate them into different groups and different sects for better understanding - i suppose. but what we loose when we do this, is we loose the feeling of togetherness - Oneness. we are all One, we flow together and interconnect. all topics, all things, that we try to materialize in our thoughts and in our consciousness as separate are one. in this society we feel that we must be unique in order to have value, but even uniqueness has a tie to something previously seen, felt, heard, thought of by another. everything flows together, everything works together. everything has a soul and everything has flow. so this is something else to think about. we all are connected we all have a flow. we are all One. all topics are one. because they come form the One consciousness. and we cannot separate them even though we may try to.*

Evening of February 28, 2013

we are ready to begin. yes yes yes. we are ready to begin. yes, sometimes it shocks you when we come into your system. we understand, we understand, we understand. yes, we are ready, we are ready to begin, we are ready to come into you. yes, there you go, there you go. adjust. adjust. adjust. feel our frequency and move into it. there you are. yes yes yes. we are ready to begin this evening. *what would you like to discuss today? (pause) what is it that you guys would like to discuss tonight? what is it? please come through me straight through me it will be much easier than me trying to analyze your information. please.* we want to discuss many things. as always we want to discuss discuss discuss. we want you to think about all the topics that we are bringing through. we want you to think about them. we want you to allow us to come into your system. yes there you go. yes, yes go deeper deeper deeper. relax relax relax relax. that's better, that's better, that's better. yes yes yes now we can come through. this is much better for us. yes very good. okay we want to discuss many things tonight. and we have many different topics that we can choose to discuss. it is up to you which ones you want to choose. *is this for the book?* (pause) yes, it is for the book.

*what do you want to talk about?* we want to talk about the influence. yes heather you are wondering what this is. you are wondering what is the influence. you are wondering what does this mean, what does this mean, what does this mean. the influence is something that has not been discussed here before. it is something that is different to this society. the influence is whatever you want to make it out to be. the influence is (pause) the influence is what you think it is. the influence is: fear, vulnerability, dissatisfaction, annoyance. (pause) yes yes yes the influence, heather, continue continue. what is it? what is it, what is it? (pause)

**the influence is whatever you choose it to be, a blockage in your life. whatever you choose to allow yourself to be blocked by and not to reach into your Divine Self, into your true self and allow that [Light] to spread to the world. the influence is whatever negative aspects that you cling to, the things such as fear, the things such as loathing, these things, these things, these things. not allowing yourself to reach the highest point that you possibly can. your highest energy level. your higher being. your true self. your One self.** yes, yes, yes, this is what we are calling the influence. the influence, the influence, heather. yes, yes, yes, this is what we are working with your system right now. when you allow these things to come into your system you are allowing the influences to occur. and when the influence, which we are talking about is many different things. whatever you choose in your system, whatever is right for you, you, you. it all depends on whatever is going on in your life. it is specific to each person. everyone has their own influence. everyone has chosen these things to allow themselves to be blocked off from what they truly are and who they truly are and why they are here - why they are here, why they are here, why they are here. so this is up to you. many people have chosen different things, different walks of life.

in the case of heather, she has chosen not to love herself truthfully, not allow yourself to fully trust. everyone has their own different blocks that they are working through. and that is why they are here on this earth, that is why we are all here to learn - learn, learn, learn. and so this is what we are working with her system right now. she is feeling a pressure between her chest as we are trying to work within her system on allowing herself to feel love, love, love, love. and allow this into her system. allow herself to feel this fully and be One with Love. and yes we want this, we want this, we want this. and so as she is doing this, as she is working with her system and we are working with her system to become One. she is feeling this pressure here, as we are moving through her. we are moving through her. we are moving through her. and we are attempting to get rid of these voids that she has in her system. anything that she has, we are trying to move through them, we are trying to allow them to acclimate.

so whatever influence it is that you have in your life. (yes, we are talking to the reader now, we are talking to you). (devon's voice) yes yes yes whatever influences you have in your life, you must let it go. you must choose to move on. you must allow it out of your system. you must choose to have it removed from your system. allow it to go, allow it to go, allow it to go. this is not to be born anymore.

you do not need this, you do not need this, you do not need this. you cling onto these things because you feel that you need them. that they will protect you. that it is safety, safety, safety. and it is not safe, it is not safe, it is not safe. we will repeat this. what you feel is safe sometimes is not safe. often times it is not safe. what is safe, and what this feeling of safety that you are focusing on, is created out of fear. you fear something so you create a safe zone for yourself. however there is no such thing as this need for fear. everyone feels this need, you do not need this fear. you do not need it, you do not need it, you do not need it.

this is what we are discussing today. you do not need your fear. you do not need these influences in your life. you do not need them, you do not need them, you do not need them. try to get rid of them, try to get rid of them, try to get rid of them. we can help you work through that, if you call upon us, if you call on us. we will come to you. any of your spirit guides anyone anyone anyone. that is from the other realm, will help you work through these, will help you through these, help you through these. bring them up to you, up front, up front, bring these up, so you realize what these are. when you realize what they are, then you can recognize them. if you do not know what the problem is, then you cannot tangle with it. you cannot allow yourself to move past it, move beyond it. because you cannot recognize it. so you have to realize what these things are. you have to realize what they are and then you can move forward, you can move forward, you can move forward. (end devon's voice) and this is what we want, this is what we want, this is what we want. we want this for everyone, we want it for everyone, we want it for everyone, we want it for everyone. we want for everyone to be able to move forward and move on in their lives and move to the next stages. we are not talking just about the physical life, but we are talking more about the spiritual

spiritual spiritual. yes yes yes. so allow these influences to be moved away from you. allow them to be moved into a different place and not obstruct you.

yes, yes, yes. heather this is what...yes, yes, yes...we want to continue, continue. yes. so, we do not want these things to come in and block your life. we do not want this, we do not want this, we do not want this. we want you to allow these things to be removed removed removed. **allow yourself to come into your safe zone, which in reality is moving outside of the safe zone that you are already in. we want you to move from these feelings of being alone, unwanted, unloved, or whatever it is.** this fear, this fear, this fear, this fear. yes heather, yes heather, yes. yes. whatever fear that it is that you are bringing into your system it is not appropriate for you. you do not need it, you do not need it, you do not need it. you can choose it. yes yes yes yes we are saying this: you can choose, you can choose, you can choose anything that you want to. you can have whatever you want, you can have whatever you want, you can have whatever you want. so we want you to decide which do you want? do you want to live your life based in fear? or do you want to live your life based in Love? when you choose Love over fear - Love conquers all. we will say this again. we have said this before and it is true. it is true, it is true. Love conquers all. allow yourself to love. allow yourself to love, allow yourself to love. allow yourself to be a conduit as they say, as they say, as they say, to be part of Love. to choose Love and "then you will bring love into your life" - (devon).

and when you bring love into your life, you bring love into other peoples' lives and they will come forward and they will come to you. yes yes yes heather, you are talking and you are thinking of the man today when you were listening to the paul selig video. and what resonated with you: is that you feel you need to shake people that are not awakened to the level that you are at and you need to shake them up and make sure they are where they need to be in life, because they are not where you are. and we are saying exactly as paul selig's guides said, "that this is not necessary. you do not need to do this, you do not need to do this, you do not need to do this." this would not be based in love. you would not be doing this out of love. you would be doing it out of the ego self. out of the self that is saying, "hey, hey, hey, hey you! you are not where I am at." and that is wrong, that is wrong, that is wrong. even if you are coming from a place of love like, "hey, come into my field, come into this." they cannot recognize that until they choose to. they must come into that system, because you are in that system. they must choose your system, they must choose what you are doing through the energy received from your system. so this is up to them, this is up to them, this is up to them. you have to choose you. you have to be centered. you have to be One. you have to choose this. and when you are that, then other people can connect with this energy and they can choose this for themselves as well. and they can come up to the level that they need to. and if they go higher than your level then you can choose their level. and this is what we are saying: this is the domino effect. the domino effect, the domino effect that we are talking about earlier. it all interconnects. everyone inter-connects, all the subjects, all the topics in the world inter-connect. somehow they all work together. and so we are saying this right now, everything works together - everything. we all work together. we all work together - people on the other side of the veil (as you see it because you cannot see us sometimes, but you will see us, you will see us, you will see us).

yes, yes, yes, yes heather. you will see us, you will see us at some point. everyone can see us. these walls will be broken down, as they need to be. as they need to be and

as people choose them to be. choosing, choosing, choosing.
when you choose to allow yourself to move beyond this
physical realm. beyond what you think is important.
beyond the things that you have been taught that are
important, you will see what truly is important. what really
matters, what really matters, what really matters. yes
heather, we know that you think that we are just repeating
information. we are not, we are not, we are not. we are
making points stronger, stronger and stronger in this book.
and we want you to realize that. we are talking about
things that need to be talked about and yes we may be
talking about them over and over again, but they will have
different energy, different energy, different energy. people
can connect with that, can connect with that, can connect
with that. so we want you to know this. so do not allow
your system to become flooded because you think that we
are not coming through you properly. we are coming
through you properly. you hear us, you feel us now. we are
coming through you very strongly. yes yes yes. you can feel
this, you can feel this, you can feel this. this is good, this is
good. yes we are coming through you as hard as we
possibly can right now because we know that your system
is tired. and we want to get all the information out that we
possibly can for this evening. so let us begin, let us begin,
let us begin.

we want to continue this discussion. we want to
move forward. we want to move forward. yes, the things
that you have been thinking about, the things that you
have brought up to your mind are exactly right. yes, you
are analyzing the difference between you and paul selig
and the information that you are presenting is not in such a
scholarly fashion. and this is exactly right. this is what we
want, this is what we want, this is what we want. we want
everyone to be able to connect with this information. we
are not saying that paul selig's information is wrong. we

are not saying that, we are not saying that, we are not
saying that. his information is very good and it is at a level
that is very good, if you are at that level. if you are at that
intellectual level. if you have reached that level here on this
plane already. however if you have not reached that level
and you have not been studying at stanford or these ivy
league schools, then you do not speak at that level. and as
you are noticing, because you thought that he was
channeling just his spirit guides, just straight through him
and he is not really, he is still integrating this information
into his system and allowing it to come through him. come
through him, come through him as a filter. just as we are
coming through you. yes, yes, yes. relationship,
relationship, relationship. he was saying that he was the
person that was allowing the information to come straight
through and that his is just a radio. this is not true. this is
not true, this is not true necessarily. he was in most parts,
but he also has the ability to analyze the information.
analyze it. analyze it and have his educational overtone
because his guides can bring forward the information at
that higher education level because paul understands the
terms and words they are using. that is why it is written in
a scholarly fashion. his guides are like him, like him, like
him. yes, this is because everyone needs this. everyone
needs guides that fit their personality, fit their needs and fit
where they are going in the future and where they are
moving to in their next step. their next step, their next step.

    so we are saying this now, your book will help others
connect with you. it will help the people of this age and this
generation connect with you. connect with you. connect
with you. and that is what we want. we want people to
realize that they can connect with anyone at any age and
they can do this [channeling] at any age. we want people to
realize this. anyone, at any age, at any stage in life, can
allow themselves to connect with people beyond and move

into this state of Oneness. into this One Consciousness and allow themselves to become One. no one is limited, no one is limited, no one is limited. no one is limited by race, gender, creed, any of these things that allow separation to occur, allow separation in the mind. allow them to put them into different sections, people, put in different sections. this is wrong, this is wrong, this is wrong. everyone is One. just because their outwardly appearance may not be one. their sex may not be one. your desires may not be one - all of the desires are One. everything is One, everything is One, everything is One, heather. yes, yes, yes. everything is One. so do not worry, do not worry, do not worry. everything is One. just because your neighbor is doing something differently than you, does not mean that it is not One - it is not part of the Oneness. they may choose it, they may choose not to be a part of the Oneness. this is up to them, this is up to them, this is up to them - this is up to you. you have to choose Oneness, you have to choose Oneness, you have to choose Oneness.

yes, yes, yes, we want you to realize this: you worry about too much sometimes; the people outside of your frequency and the people that you maybe can not effect right now. we want you to focus on you. when you to focus on you, this is true for the reader. when you focus on you, when you focus on you, when you focus on you, the whole entire world changes around you. things conform to the things that you need. if you are focusing on love, if you are focusing on love, you attract love, you attract love, you attract love. and so this is what we want you to realize: when you change, the world changes. when you change, the world changes. people come to you. they are attracted to you like moths to the flame. is something that heather was thinking about earlier. when you become the flame, The Light, The Light, The Light. yes, yes, yes all the people come to it. and they allow themselves to be soaked

up into this and allow themselves to move up in the higher
energy field. yes, yes, yes, yes. higher energy, higher
energy, higher energy. yes, this is up to them, this is up to
them, this is up to them. so what we are saying for the
reader and for yourself. is that you must focus on you. and
we are not talking about egotistically. we are not saying,
"oh yes, I must focus on me because i am the most
important person in the world." in a way yes you are. but
not an egotistical way, we are not trying to stroke the ego
here. we are saying that you are the most important person
in the world, in the fact that you have to get yourself into a
loving state, into a loving manner and allow yourself to
allow this to be given to other people. when you fill
yourself up, then you can over flow and fill others up as
well. and so we are saying this starts with you. it starts
with one and then it can spread to many. so the Oneness
starts with one and then it spreads to many and this all
becomes One. so this is what we are trying to say. this
concept is difficult for most. most people can't really
understand it and so we try to bring this around:

so heather is seeing herself as a glass and as she is filled up,
filled up, filled up, filled up. everyone is in the sink and
they can be filled up as well. so as she slowly fills up and
everything pours out and over. this is filled up into other
peoples glasses, other peoples glasses and other peoples
glasses. as people are filled up, in turn, they can do the
same for others and it is this domino, ripple effect,
compounding, compounding...yes, you are thinking
compounding interest. yes, this is the same where it slowly
builds, builds and builds. and anyone that has studied this
fact, will know what compounding interest is and what it
means. and how fascinating, how interesting and how
powerful this really is. so we want you to see this, to see
this, to see this. this is also part of what we are trying to

say tonight. this information is so powerful, so powerful, as long as, it is grabbed onto, as long as it is taken in, as long as you appreciate this information. you allow it to come through you and breathe through you and touch other people through your love. they will come in and they will be part of the love. and this will continue on as a ripple effect, a ripple effect, ripple effect, as you are seeing it.

yes, yes, yes, this is good heather, yes, yes, yes. continue. continue. yes, we can understand you are getting tired we can tell, we can tell, we can tell. but we still have more information that needs to come through tonight. yes, yes, yes, yes. we understand that you get tired at night, but you need to allow yourself to do these sessions earlier, so that you do not tax your system as much and we know that you are not feeling well. but that is okay, that is okay, that is okay. we are coming through and we are compensating for this. so do not worry, do not worry, do not worry. you will not feel taxed, you will feel as if you have been having a weight lifted off of you with this information coming through you. do not worry, do not worry, do not worry. (breathing) yes, very good allow your system to relax for a moment heather. yes, allow it, allow it, allow it.

(pause)

yes, yes, we want to continue on. we want to continue on with the idea of the influences. the things that you allow into your system that do not need to be there. the things that you think are very important. like having the fancy car. having the great house, having the trophy wife/husband - everything that is "keeping up with the jonses." this is not important, this is not important, this is not important. you think it is, you think it is, you think it is because everyone else around you is striving for these

things. however. not everyone is striving for them. you see
this in your system because this is what you want to see;
this is what you want to believe. and so this is what you
see. and in return this is all there is. but in reality, there are
many people searching for different things out there. there
are many people content with where they are in life. many
people searching through spiritual changes, they want
changes and they want them in different ways. and they
are realizing that all of these physical objects, although
great in many ways, are also a way to hold yourself down
and tie yourself to one place and not allow your true self
and your spiritual self to come through. so we want people
to realize this as well. and this may come as a shock to
many people. because especially if they realize, "well we
can have anything we want. we can have anything we
should choose. we can have it, we can have it, we can have
it." well yes, you can have it. you can choose it, you can
have it in your system. and we are not saying that these
things are bad. we are saying that when you become
completely monopolized by all of this stuff that you have to
have and tied down by it and feel that this is security, this
is security, this is security. no. this is not security, you are
secure when you are in Love. you are secure when you feel
yourself in this state of Love. and you know that you are
loved by the one true God. and that this person and this
being, will come and help you at any time and at any point,
and this is what we can say is true about us, we come from
the source of Love. we come from the source of Love, we
come from the source of Love, as do you. as do you. you
think that you are separate from this, but you are not. you
are all part of the Oneness, you are part of the Oneness,
you are part of the Oneness. yes. heather wants to talk
about her first experience when she decided to open up to
channel and we will discuss this now, or we will allow her
to discuss this now:

so yes, i guess one of these things that i wanted to talk about was when i first opened up to allowing my guides to verbally communicate through me. my very first channeling experience was very emotional, because you are allowing them to come into your system. you can feel them much more easily [as apposed to internal channeling]. the information that was coming through was amazing and awe inspiring. the feeling that i received as becoming part of the Oneness, becoming connected with them, and that they were never really gone (which is what you feel when you haven't fully connected with them by verbally channeling) was overtaken by this feeling of Oneness. that we have been one and that we will always be one.

my initial instinct, or feeling, was that i had been held outside of The Light. that i had not been allowing this experience, that i was holding myself back and in reality this was true. i was choosing this. i was assured by the feeling of knowing that they were never gone. they have always been there, they have always been loving me. love is always here, it is always tangible. whatever you want is always here. **you have to choose it. and we always come back to this choice, choice, choice, everyday. every single thing you do, every feeling you choose to have - you are choosing it. in response you may be saying, "sometimes you can not love. if i am slapped in the face of course that is going to trigger anger instinctually."** well not for everyone. some people cry instead. so you are choosing whatever feeling is coming to the surface. and you are either choosing to allow it to take control over your body, mind, system, for however long or you can choose Love. you can choose to turn the other cheek. you can choose to allow yourself to be the person you want to be - the loving, caring, kind, tender person. so allowing yourself to do this and choosing this for your system is very important. you have always had this choice. you have never been held outside of The Light. you are never not part of the Oneness. you may feel that way and this is because you have chosen to feel that

*way. this is basically what i wanted to share with you, with my*
*beginning experience. that everything is full of choices, chalked full*
*of them all day long. it is nothing but a nice barrel of choices. haha!*
*so i just wanted to share that part of that experience with you.*

yes, this is good heather. yes, of course we will have
some editing to do. do not worry. do not worry. do not
worry. just allow the information to come. you know this,
you know this, you know this. yes, yes, yes. so we want
you to realize that we are bringing forth the information
that we want you to bring in. this is a duality, a duality, a
duality. this is a relationship. we do not want people that
do not have a relationship with their guides to think we
only come through them [the channeler], rather there is a
relationship there. we do not want a fully channeled text
because we do want your ideas and your thoughts to come
through as well. and these are coming through your higher
self often times and they are coming through your need to
bring information out into the light. into the light. into the
light. and this is all good, this is all good, this is all good.
yes, yes, yes.

(pause)

yes, yes, yes we want to discuss the title of the book.
yes we like that you are talking about being the closet
channeler. yes we like this, we like this, we like this. yes,
we want the picture of you to be on the front cover and we
can see it now. yes yes we think this will be good with you
on the front cover with the door open and yes yes in your
room or with the hands. where it is, where it is right now,
where you are channeling and showing this area, showing
this. and allowing people to open up, allowing these blocks
to come down. privacy. the things that people think they
need to keep out from everyones view. everyone can feel

everyone else's thoughts and secrets - everything. they can feel them, they know them [other's thoughts]. whether or not they can recognize them and verbalize them is a different story. but they can feel them, they can know them. so there is nothing to hide, nothing to hide, nothing to hide. there are no worries, no worries, no worries. so allow yourself to just be open to everyone and they will be open to you. this is what you want, this is what you want, this is what you want. *yes, yes, yes okay*... (pause) yes we can feel that you are tired. we can see this, we can see this, we can see this, we can see this. it is time to be done. you can stop, goodnight and thank you for everything you have done today.

# Chapter Twelve

## Failing

Morning of March 1, 2013

let us begin. we are happy with what was achieved yesterday and we are ready to begin, we are ready to begin, we are ready to begin. let us begin, let us begin, let us begin. let us put in what we need to put in this book today. let us talk about the things that you have learned last night. let us continue. let us continue. we would like to discuss. (pause) we would like to discuss failings. *is that correct guys? failings.* yes, yes, yes. we want to discuss failings; we want to discuss this. we want to discuss what failing means to other people. we want to discuss how people feel about this. everyone thinks that they fail in life. everyone has to judge everything against one another. everyone has to have doubt. everyone has to have fear. everyone has to have this feeling of blame. and this is what we want to talk about this feeling of failings: there is no such thing as failing. there is only learning, learning,

learning, learning. people view certain things as learning the wrong way. that is not true. there is no wrong way of learning. there are harder ways sometimes of learning. but this is what you have to go through sometimes. this is the process that you have to go through in order to learn and learn and learn and bring yourself higher. so this is just different for each person. especially when they are not connected so much with their guides, where they would be able to get assistance and guidance from beyond.

so we do not look at anyone and we do not judge them. you judge yourself. you choose this. you choose to judge yourself and evaluate what you have come from. there is no reason to blame yourself though, for anything that you have done or anything you have chosen. there is only evaluation. there is discernment of whether or not you would do that again for yourself or whether you would want that for someone else. this is what we are talking about: discerning, discerning, discerning. but there is no such thing as failing. you do not fail in any process. you have many lives to live. if you "fail" then you can choose to do this over again in the next life. there is no such thing as failing.

this is where we think that you should be taking chances. allow yourself to move outside of your box, to move outside of your comfort zone. move, move, move. become the things that you want, do the things that you want and allow yourself that freedom. when you allow yourself that freedom. there is no such thing as failing because you are doing everything with love. you are doing everything with excitement, passion. and you are allowing yourself to move beyond these principles, these walls of failing.

*tom edison didn't think he failed. he didn't think he failed. when he couldn't figure out the light bulb on the first one or the hundredth one. no, he didn't think he failed. he just found one-hundred ways in which not to make a light bulb. and thats okay. some of the greatest people in the world do not view failing as failing. instead they view it as an opportunity to succeed. what people viewed as wrong, he got right in the end. it just took him longer to do these things that some were thinking. persistence, persistence, persistence and knowing and believing that something will happen and that you are on the right path is what it is all about.*

and we want to say this again, this is what this is all about. yes, yes, yes, yes. you are here to learn, you are here to learn. you are here to learn. we want you to break outside of your box. we want you to move beyond these walls that you have put yourself in, that people have put themselves in. and we want them to break outside of these walls and move beyond it. choose the things that you love to do. choose the things you have passion for. choose the things you have momentum for. choose, choose, choose. do not allow yourself to become stuck. do not allow yourself to shut down. do not allow yourself to become bored. do not allow this. do not allow this, do not allow this. **if whatever you are doing currently in your life you find boring, you find repetitious and you find that you are not doing the things that you want to be doing - move beyond this. move beyond this. allow yourself to become creative. allow yourself to tap into your creative loving source and allow yourself to move beyond it [the boredom].** when you do this, you will find that there is a world out there, a world beyond whatever you could ever imagine. that will be here for whatever you want to do. whatever you want to do in life. and just because you may have your eye set on something that has to be done a certain way. you may change your mind. and it may come about in a totally different way. it is not for you to worry about the how. it is for you to worry about the what. what is it that you like to do? **truly ask yourself, what is it that you like to do? what is it that you want to do in the future? it can be a broad subject: it can be i want to help people. it can be i want to bring unity in this world. then choose to do the things that will help people bring unity.** we want you to realize that you can have broad things that you want to do and you can achieve them. you can allow yourself to make this and we want you to choose these things. when you choose these things people are so worried about, "well i can't. there isn't any money in that, i can't do this, i can't do that." all of that is a creation. and you are choosing it. when you are saying, "i can't, i can't, i can't." well guess what. you're right, you can't. choose you can, you can, you can and you will. **choose it, move through it and do it.** we will be here to help you through the paths. things may have to change, you may see them as road blocks. they are not road blocks, they are things that you need to learn, you need to learn, you need to learn or you need to move beyond. this is what this life is here for, for you to learn, learn, learn, learn. move beyond the things that you think you can and can't do and just do them. do what you want to do in this life. this is why you are here, this is why you are here, this is why you are here.

so we want you to do the things that you want to do out of love, out of compassion. when you do that, there is no wrong. all the energy in the world will work with you; in order for you to get to where you need to go. so this is very important, this is very important, this is very important. people will be allowed to do the things that people want to do. they will be more than allowed, they will be moved in the direction of achieving these things. how they want them to occur is again not their worry. but they will occur and they will be happy. **have your end dream goal and allow yourself to move in that direction.** we want you to love, love, love, love. unconditionally love everything around you and love what you are doing.

this is important for you to love thyself. when you start loving thy self, you stop doing all these things that you think you need to do and you start doing the things you want to do. the things that bring you joy, the things that make you happy. when you choose the things that make your inner-self happy, others will crowd around you and help make your dreams come true. this is the way the world works. we want people to realize this: love, love, love is the key to everything and there is no such thing as failing. there is no such thing as failing. even if you choose not to do the things that you love and you choose to be stuck. we do not view that as a failing. we will accept you in whatever form you are. we will accept you for whoever you choose to be and whoever you think you are. even if you choose not the true self. that is fine. we except you in love and we do not judge any of your behavior. you must choose what you want in this life and what you want moving forward. up to you, up to you, up to you. choose, choose, choose, choose.

so we want to re-enforce this again. there is no such thing as failing. everyone is worried about failing, failing, failing. what is this concept of failing? *the concept of failing is when you view the people outside of you and they tell you, you are failing. so your view of failing is an out-picturing of what other people are going to think. so you have already created these road blocks in your mind that you are going to fail and you hold onto that and it comes true because you have given it your energy. by latching onto that, you have allowed it to come into the core-self and you have chosen failing. but when you take a different mental picture. you take a different way of viewing things, as thomas edison did with the light bulb. and you choose this picture, you will be choosing success. you will be choosing to have whatever it is and hold it in your hands and have it working the way you want it to work. when you choose this, you love this image and you don't allow these*

*other 'failings' to creep in and you come from your place of knowing.*
**you will have success.**

success we are talking about is love, love, love. if you have something that moves you and you move forward in passion, in love and watch what will happen. we promise amazing things, we promise miracles. we promise change in life. we promise, we promise, we promise. everything here on this earth, everything that you see in front of you is an out-picturing of what you have chosen in life. so if you see yourself as a failure or a success, this is an out-picturing of what you have chosen in your life. we want you to realize that everything is controlled by you. by you, by you, by you. we aren't saying that there aren't jerks in this world and there aren't people that purposely try and spite you. but this is a test. now what do you choose? love or anger? choose love. they are there for you to learn a lesson. choosing love, will move you forward into The Light. you will become at peace with yourself and there will be no need for these thoughts of failure.

so this is what we want to leave you with today. yes, yes, yes. we want to leave you with, there is no such thing as failing. only things that you are thinking of as failings and that is up to you. we also want to say anything can be a success out there, you have to choose, you have to move in love for your Divine Desire and it will bring you peace and joy. everything is controlled by Love. failing is only what you want it to be. yes there are road blocks every once in a while, but these are only lessons and directions. allow your mental picturing to change like thomas edison and realize how unlimited you and this universe can be - choose it. we thank you very much for your time here heather and we appreciate you going through this information today. we look forward to discussing more this evening. we love you very much. have a wonderful day. thank you. you may stop now. *thank you, love you.*

# Chapter Thirteen

## Love and Creation

Morning of March 3, 2013

we must begin. we must begin. yes, there you go, there you go. this is much better. allow yourself to relax, relax, relax. let us continue today. we would like to speak about...today we would like to speak about love and creation. yes, you are thinking that we are copying paul selig. we are not, we are not, we are not. we are copying what is already known and what everyone already knows. we are just saying it in a different way. so love and creation is what we want to speak about today. everyone is in love and everyone comes from Love. everyone must be Love. so this must be a realization that everyone must come from. they must allow themselves to be woken up and to love. and allow this to come into their hearts and into their minds. allow this to be projected to others as it is unto them. when you become the well for love, you become the well for others to also drink

from. when you become this, you become what the whole
world needs; which is more love, more love, more love. yes,
you are thinking about the beatles' song. yes. enlighten,
enlightened, enlightened. they had some abilities of
enlightenment that they were getting through their work.
yes, yes, yes. everyone has this, everyone has this,
everyone has this. source of enlightenment. this is up to
them how much they choose in their life and how they
choose to go forward and if they choose this or choose to
block it or try to control it. which is up to them. up to
them, up to them.

(pause)

    yes you must allow the waters of your mind to calm.
you must allow us to come through. very good. yes. you
feel that you have touched on this topic before and that we
are discussing the same things over and over again. but we
are saying love is the most important thing - that it must be
discussed over and over again. in different forms and in
different ways for people to connect with it, connect with
the material, connect with this and move forward. so this is
important, this is important, this is important. we must
bring this information through in many different forms, in
many different ways for people to connect in different
forms and allow themselves to realize that they are the
source of love. and when they are the source of love and
realize that they have control, they have the power to
choose love, that when they choose love, they can be love
and they can be the fountain of love and they can be love
for others and they will only see love and this is what we
want. so yes. there are different ways of talking about the
subject; there are different ways of connecting to it.
because their are different energies, different energies, and
everyone connects to energies differently. everyone comes

into a different energy source differently. they are allowed to connect with it, on different levels of themselves and their being.

you are speaking this information, you are allowing it to come through you heather. yes, yes, yes allow it to come through. this means that you are allowing different forms of Love to come through your body and allow it to become part of the reader. when the reader is reading this, they will connect with things differently. some will not connect with some of the information, and others will. but once they have come to the higher level, to a higher understanding, to their Divinity. they will understand and they will become part of Love and they will choose Love and they will be the well of Love. when everyone is the well of Love, this world will be filled with Love and filled with Light. there will be no more fear, no more fear, no more fear. everything will move beyond this. and this is what we want to discuss today. everything will move beyond this level of fear that surrounded this earth - through Love. Love conquers all. we have said this before, it is very important. Love is what everyone needs in order to move forward; in order to move into their next level of consciousness, their next level of Oneness. when you love everyone, everyone must love you. and in return, you will receive more love than you could ever think of. and this is what we want everyone to realize. everyone has this ability to become loved and they are Love, they are part of Love, they have all the love that they need already.

"you already possess everything necessary to become great" - native american, crow proverb. *you have everything in this earth and everything around you to create what you want. you have everything that you have ever needed and this is up to you to choose it.* we again go back and hark to choice, choice, choice. you have the ability to choose whatever you want and whatever you want to see around you.

heather is working with this material already. she is realizing she must choose what life it is that she wants to have. she must choose her outlook on life. even though she may have things come into her life, and this is also part of her out-picturing, that she may not like. she can choose them and not give them energy and move beyond them and think of something good. when you think of the something good, you give it love. rather than giving that energy to something that is negative - you choose Love. and this is what we are talking about again with choosing Love and creating from Love. when you choose, when you choose love rather than the negativity that you can see out there in the world, that you can choose from, you are choosing to only create from Love. so when you have a choice and something comes upon you and you choose the loving creative aspect of it, which can be hard in some cases, you are choosing to come from Love and be apart of the well of Love. and this is what we want, this is what we want, this is what we want. yes, heather share what you want to share:

*okay well, what they are trying to hark back to with this example this morning: it was my sisters birthday today and everyone was a little moody. i don't know, people get moody around other peoples birthdays for whatever reason. i think there is this level of expectation or something. basically my dad was getting upset with my sister who was in the bathroom and taking a long while, some silly drama. and he came up and his whole energy was very negative and was affecting both my mom and myself. and we were talking about it and giving it more energy and getting upset about it. and then i realize and it clicked in that i am not creating from Love. i am creating from fear or this place that is not from a source of Love. if i was in a source of Love, i would drop the topic and move on. because it is his issue for him to handle, not mine and not my moms. and once i brought that up to my mom and said no we need to decided for right now we are not going to discuss it. we are going to move on. we are not going to discuss it and move onto a better, more positive topic. which we did and all the sudden the energy and the negativity that was going on in that situation deflated and moved away from us and we didn't have to deal with any of it.*

so this is exactly what we are talking about. when you are creating from Love. what people only see is Love and a source of Love and this will create peace and harmony. because you are living in the now. so you are living now and you are allowing yourself to feel the love, even if there are negative things going on around you. and allowing yourself to feel love for another person or thing. and allow yourself in a way to become distracted from the negative sources coming into your life. once you choose that and constantly come from a place of Love, you will never ever ever see or deal with this place a fear or negativity that is out there. that others are choosing and when you choose that, others can come to your energy and can choose it as well. *and this is what they are talking about. you become the well of Love. when you choose this, you become this. and others will choose to align to yours or they will not. but you will not have to deal with them. they do not enter your energy source. they will not be in your line of site. and they will not affect you. this is very important and this is a total change of how you deal in your daily life, because it is so easy (at least for me) to become wrapped up in these little negative things: this didn't go the exact way i wanted it to or that didn't. therefore i am going to be upset and hold a grudge all day long and i am going to be spiteful. well that only gives you more of that same energy. which i do not want for the rest of my life. i don't want to be spiteful and come from a place of lack. place of fear. place of negativity. i want to come from a place of Love, and have others feel that, and have others choose that as well. and then live in a world that is based in love and based in positivity.*

*so this is something that you need to decide to choose from.*

*and it is not as easy as it sounds. these books are written, all these books on the market out there proclaim that if you do this then you will get this. but no, there is feeling, emotion, there is a conscious decision to choose these things. when you are choosing them, you are giving them energy and you are allowing them to fill you up and really allow yourself to consciously choose the effort to come from the place of Love. and once you do that it becomes, like they are saying, the domino effect of being easily triggered into, "ahh i need to choose love here. i need to be choosing a different path. i need to be choosing love." then you will automatically see the turn around. love, love, love, love, love but this all comes from choice. and this is what they want us to do. at least this is my belief - is this correct?* yes, this is correct heather. *that everyone if they choose love and get to this place of Love, will choose this Love for everyone else. it can be done. if you can do it, i can do it. everyone else will be choosing Love and it will be a cycle of Love, love, love, love. we will be One in Love. when we are One in Love then we will be One together, One Consciousness, one unite, one feeling, one vibration moving forward together, for everyone together as One. and this is very powerful.　this is something very different from where we have come from. we have been creating from this place of fear and separation, control and we have allowed that to take over our lives and change us into not loving our neighbor and not loving thyself. and when we do this, we loose ourselves. we loose who we are and we loose who others are and we expect them to fill us up with this love. instead of allowing ourselves to be filled up from our inner love, allow ourselves to be loved and then in turn love others and they will love us in return as well. when you realize that, the source of Love is from within and when you create from it you become the well and you allow others to connect to this and allow others to drink from it. then you will receive nothing else but love from others and from the world. love from the One. that is what they are trying to say here and that is what they are trying to come to. yes they are saying (as i keep getting semi-annoyed with them) that they are repeating this over and over in different ways, because they want people to connect with this information and realize what they are saying how important this is to our lives. so we can connect with it. and every day they show me different ways of doing this. and your guides can show you the different ways to do this as well. as you start choosing this and you start choosing this source. you will become connected with this source around you and you will make a conscious effort to choose Love, become Love, drink from the well of Love, be Love, and choose One. domino effect, domino effect, domino effect.*

yes, yes, this is good heather. yes, yes, yes, this is very good. we want you to continue with sharing the examples that come up in your head, because this is very important for the reader. the reader must be able to understand these things because they must be able to connect, connect, connect. you are One. you all have experiences to allow you to connect with each other. which allow you to understand each others' wisdom and what is coming through the energy level. when you connect with one another you are allowing yourself to share and share in Love. share this experience. share this knowledge. share this learning and become Love. and this is what we want, this is what we want, this is what we want.

yes, you are thinking back to the native americans again. which has been a good influence in your life, as far as this book and what you think of. and you are thinking about yes, how they share stories, stories, stories. yes, this whole entire world has different stories that have different truths to them and this is wisdom as we call it. the wisdom will carry you through, carry you to were you need to go. this is very important. you must allow this. you must allow this. you must allow this. you must allow all this information around you to come into your system and digest in Love and then you will be able to project your love and share your knowledge and allow yourself to connect with them and share with them through experiences. through stories. this is what has been done, has been done. has been done    -through history and throughout time. it will continue. it will continue. it will continue. stories are important. stories are important. stories are important. this is what everyone needs. this is how everyone connects together. this is how we connect energy, through stories. this is how we learn - through stories. this is how it will always be; this is how it will be done. whether the communication level is different, whether it is telepathically. whether it is through verbal, as you are doing now. it will always be through stories, that the information will be learned the best. it will come in through the system. it will be synthesized. it will come in. it will come in. it will come in. and people will understand this and they will allow this information to come into their system and they will allow it to be shared with others. and this is good. this is good. this is good. this is what we want. everyone has this ability. everyone has it. everyone has it. no one is better than anyone else. everyone is the same. everyone has all these gifts. whether they choose them is up to them. choice, choice, choice, choice. we will hark back to this every single day. choice, choice, choice - it matters.

choices will define you. they will tell you where you are in life. they will let you know what is going on around you, through your choices. they will come back to you and they will show themselves in the out-picturing of what you see going on around you. this is what we want you to know. your choices have made your world around you. they will continue to make your world around you. if you come from a place of love and you choose love, then your world around you will be surrounded by nothing but love. again, again, again. choose love and you will be choosing love. you will be choosing knowledge. you will be choosing a future full of this for everyone else around you. this is what we want. this is what we want. this is what we want. this is what we want. (pause) this is good. this is good. this is good. yes, this information is what we wanted. yes, this is very good heather. yes. *is there anything else you want to talk about today?* love does not fear. love does not hate. love does not worry. love does no wrong. love is forever. love is choice. choose love. thank you heather and we will stop. God bless. love you. *love you too, guys. name of the Father, Son and Holy Spirit. amen.*

# Chapter Fourteen

## Love and Logic

*there is no such thing as privacy. we are all here, we are all One. what you hold in the dark will come to the light, we know each others' secrets. "therefore whatsoever ye have spoken in darkness shall be heard in the light; and that which ye have spoken in the ear in closets shall be proclaimed upon the housetops." Luke 12:3 King James Bible (Cambridge, Ed.) let us not be afraid, but rather embrace and proclaim the truth inside our hearts. we all know each others' secrets, their is safety in Love.*

Evening of March 3, 2013

(prior to this, my guides and i discussed personal matters. they wanted the following short chapter to be included in the book).

allow yourself to come from a place of love and then allow yourself to dissolve what you see as issues. when you look at issues through the lens of Love things change, things move, they do not look the same. they do not appear the same. they do have the same energy. because your frequency, coming out from you, is Love. so all that it can receive into its' frequency is a state of Love. you are seeing this green bubble lens come around you, this is good, this is good, this is good. when you are bringing that energy out there, you are creating almost a force field, as you are seeing it, around you. that is the flow of Love and all you can attract into it is the flow of Love. so this is exactly what you need to understand: when you are choosing love, these other things that you see as issues will no longer appear, because they are not in that state, in a congruence with Love. so everything ties in together; everything equals the same thing. it is the same reaction that you receive...you are just thinking of something. yes, you are thinking every action has an equal and opposite reaction. yes, yes, yes, yes, good.

this is what we want you to realize, bring in all these things that you know and allow this to flow and allow this to come in. people understand these terms when you use them, because they have heard them before. and can react with them and bring them into their energy field and this can be love, love, love. and this can be knowing. so yes this is what we are talking about with energy. we are talking about with everything you put out, you get back in return. equal or quadruple depending on the strength that goes out. when you choose Love, you choose unconditional Love, you receive this back. we aren't saying that there aren't some karmatic things that might arise that you may have to work through. once you work through these karmatic issues you will come to this place of enlightenment. you will come to this place of knowing. you will come to this place of Love and this is all you will see, all you will see, all you will see. we promise, we promise, we promise, we promise. so we want you to do this, we want you to allow yourself to come into the place of Love. allow yourself to be wrapped in Love, as we did earlier. allow yourself to be wrapped in this blanket. allow yourself to feel the weight of this comfortable blanket, allow yourself to feel this love come into you. relax with it. become one with it. allow yourself to be at peace.

(pause as i do this)

*this is interesting because as i am holding this invisible blanket, i am actually holding my hands as if i have a blanket wrapped around me and this was done unconsciously - very interesting. goodnight, love you. amen.*

they were just telling me, yes heather everything comes through a state of Love. everything is focused in Love. energy from Love. this is how science will figure it out. this is how science will figure it out. this is how science will figure it out. everything is attracted, everything is surrounded in Love, in Love, in Love. *and by it, i am guessing God's existence will be proven. is this correct?* yes, this is correct. *so yeah, interesting.*

closing commentary: my guides wanted me to include this information here from several weeks later during the transcription of the book, "things that are equal to the same thing are equal to each other." - euclid's mathematical law. people of all races and religions are equal to one other because they are human and therefore, One.

# Chapter Fifteen

## Chakras

Morning of March 4, 2013

*just thought of something very interesting with the chakras because i see them as expanded around the world now, rather than only in my closet, or room, or house. i want to think more universally that we are all connected, rather than limiting it to spatially. when i am beginning to channel, i first open all of my chakras and visualize them as expanding colors from their distinct areas. in the order of crown down to the root chakra: amethyst purple, dark blue (i think of the color of dark jeans), light blue, green, yellow, orange, red and brown.*

*while doing this today i stubbled upon how interesting the hierarchy (for lack of a better word) of the chakras is in relation to the earth and spiritual world. first, you have your crown chakra which is heavenly, it involves our connection to the One Consciousness - the meeting of minds. second, you have your third eye (clairvoyance) chakra, where we all can see the same things - mostly in relation to the spiritual world. thirdly, you have the voice chakra, which is when we all speak the same thing - truth - usually from our higher-selves. next, the heart chakra - our center, our Love for one another both earthly and spiritual. fifth and sixth, the upper digestive and lower digestive chakras where we all eat and digest food - more heavily related to our earthly existence. followed by the sexual gland chakra where we re-incarnate; connecting us and our future generations to this earthly existence through the gift of Spirit. And I like to think of their being an eight chakra, the root chakra (bound ankle) which connects our feet and body to this earth - grounding us.*

*we as humans have polar ends, that when perfectly balanced connect us to both the earth and our spiritual realm. we are both here, nor there. as a human we are centered in both realms through Love.* yes, yes, yes, heather continue. we are coming through you, because we want you to know that you are speaking the truth and what is coming through you is good so continue. *this is interesting how this all flows and i am starting to understand this more and more as i get into this. it was hard for me to understand the chakras at first. i didn't get what was going on there, i didn't understand it. all i knew is that once i opened them i was able to speak. i was able to get the visual aspect of it, but now i feel that i am able to move beyond the visual and connect to what is actually going on and what these flows mean. the connection of this energy and the positioning. i hope the break down will help others to understand the chakras better as well. because i think the concept is a little esoteric and hard to understand initially. hopefully this visual and understanding will help others to be able to connect with their guides through opening their chakras. lets see if the guides have anything else.*

yes, we would like to speak. yes, that was very good heather. we want you to be able to synthesize the information that is coming through. yes, these enlightened moments that are coming through you...yes, these are your higher-self and they are also us coming through, telling you the information that you need to know - need to understand, not only for yourself, but the readers will be able to understand this too. they will be able to connect with this information on an energy level and on a knowledge based level which is Knowing, Knowing, Knowing, Knowing. they will know the truth. they will know the information in truth. and they will be able to synthesize that information and bring that into their system and allow themselves to connect with what you are going through. and bring themselves up to that level as well. so this is important. this is important. this is important. and this is good, this is good, this is good.

yes, you are wondering about whether these topics you have been thinking about before should come into this book - they should, they should, they should. we want this book to be a relationship, as we said in the very beginning. we want people to realize we are coming through you. yes, coming through you, but you are also interpreting them in your own ways and you have your own information coming through and you are processing it in your mind and in your head what is going on. and this is important for other people to realize this - for other people to understand that this channeling is a process, is a relationship of understanding the material. we may be the teacher, you are the student and you will rise to a different level and at some point you can become the teacher and others will be the student. this is up to you. this is up to you. this is up to you. but we want people to understand that we are not just coming through, we are not delegating, we are not saying this is the way it must be. we are not saying that when we come through you, that you are automatically changing and that you are coming into these realizations as we speak them. so we want people to understand that this is also for you to work through, just as it is for them to work through.

nothing comes easily or overnight and in most cases we want people to realize there is a conscious level of work here that has to come through. and then when you are consciously coming through this information, you are allow it to come into your system, you are working through it in Love. then this is what we want. this is what we want. this is what we want. you will move to the next level, the next level, the next level, the next level.

you will be able to understand higher level of information that is coming through. you will be able to synthesize information. you will become more creative as you have been heather, as you have, as you have. and you know this because you have tapped into your creative Christed-Self and (devon's voice) you have allowed this to come through you. you have allowed it. you have allowed it. you have allowed it. and so since you have allowed this information to come through, you are allowing yourself to become part of the Christed-State. you are allowing Love in your life and you are allowing yourself to choose this Love and you are allowing it to become part of Love for other people. and this is important. this is important. this is important. we want people to understand this. we want people to choose the Christed-State if they want to move into this higher level. when they are choosing to allow themselves to come into this Loving state and into this energy flow, and into this state, they will be able to work through this information even more quickly (end).

rather than doing it through their mind and through their brain; they will be working through it through an energy level. they will be working through it, through a Christed-State. they will be working through it at a higher energy level, at a higher being level. this is what we want people to understand: when they allow themselves to come into the state of being in Love with thyself, then they can allow themselves to work through this information much more easily. and it will come through more easily and they will synthesize it more easily. so we understand that at a certain level people can't do this right away. unless they choose it. unless they choose it. unless they choose it. unless they choose it. they must accept the information and move it into their system and into their energy flow and then they will have this information and be working with it at a constant level. they can choose. they can choose. they can choose. they can choose. **choose yourself at a higher-state, then you will be allowing yourself to have the information come through you at that level. you will be able to work through it and you will learn the lessons in your daily life that you need to learn, but at a much faster level.** as paul selig was saying. yes, now you understand. now you understand. now you understand, yes.

*so, yeah...interestingly when i was reading paul selig's book I was like, "why isn't it just working? why isn't it doing what it needs to do?" and it is working and all his things that he has you go through in his book allow you to break through some of the energy barriers that you have. one of them in particular is the truth one. you proclaim this decree that his guides have set forward. and when you proclaim it and you allow the energy and you believe it - it really does work. one of them specifically that i am speaking about is the truth one. when i proclaimed that decree, it became very hard for me to lie or even to tell a slight version of what is not the truth. so if i say something like, "oh, she didn't do this exactly that way." then i would re-evaluate. well she did do part of this, but she didn't do this one thing. and then i would ask, why does that bother me? i would have liked it done this way and the reason for that is this. you start analyzing all this information/energy you are putting out there. and why you are saying the things the way that you used to and you start saying things differently or not at all. you are now allowing a truth state, a Divine state, you are not fearing saying something false nor allow yourself to say something in a way that isn't true.*

*you also aren't fearing this like, "oh no. i am going to be struck down by God if i don't say the truth." that is not it. when you are in this energy system and you are only going to speak the truth - you are coming from a Loving state. you do not allow the fear of whatever that lie/truth was going to be to come over you. you just say the truth as it is. if someone doesn't like it and doesn't accept it then, whatever. then you accept the possible consequences of the truth - if there are any. often times people go, "oh okay. no big." and they move beyond it. (negative out-comes are what we created in our thought process). we stop lying. not that i was big into lying anyways. i've always been overly honest. so this hasn't been a real big issue for me. but it is learning to rephrase things so that they represent the exact truth to the best of my abilities and not fearing how others will think, feel and act when they hear the truth.*

this is good. this is good. heather. yes, you are allowing yourself to have the information flow through you. you are allowing yourself to become One with this information. you are allowing it. you are allowing it. you are are allowing it. you are choosing it. and this is what we want. this is what we want. this is what we want. when you are choosing to allow this information through, you are allowing it to come through. it is not arrogant and egotistical like you think it is. you are thinking, "oh man, i am talking about myself and how awesome this book is going to be and how it is going to be a stepping stone for other people." or whatever it is you are thinking. this is not true. this is not true. this is not true. you are not being egotistical, you are actually coming from a state of Love and you are allowing this to come through and other people will see this for what it is. they will believe it is one thing or they will believe it as the other. that is their choice. we want you to realize this, everyone has a choice to come through this information, seek this information and synthesize it in their own way. react with it in their own way and then speak with it in their own way. this is up to them. this is up to them. this is up to them. they must choose. they must choose. they must choose. *okay is there anything else that we should be talking about today?* no, we think this is it. it is time to stop. we appreciate your work today and we thank you. we will be speaking with you later this evening. *thank you.*

# Chapter Sixteen

# Freedom and Out-Picturing

Evening of March 4, 2013

we are ready to begin, heather, we are ready to begin. *are we going to talk about the book today?* yes, we are going to talk about the book today. yes, we are. yes, we are. yes, we are. we must continue on with this book. we must get this done. we must get this done. we must get this done. *do you know when we will have this done by?* soon. very soon. *any date in particular?* no date yet. it depends on you, on you, on you, on you. you must decide when this will be finished. you must decide how much time and effort you are going to put into it everyday. you must decide. you must decide. you must decide. this is always up to you. you can choose whatever you want to do. if you want to get this done more quickly, then you do this twice a day. if you do not then it will be longer, it will be longer. but this is up to you. this is up to you. this is up to you. *makes sense. so what do you want to talk about today?* freedom. we want to talk about freedom.

we want to talk about what it means. what it feels like. yes, this is good heather. yes, this is good. allow yourself to relax. allow us to come in as you go more deeply. this is very good. this is very good. allow us to come in. yes, very good. very good.

yes, so we want to continue on freedom. we want to talk about this; we want to get this through. we want to start on this tonight. this is a very important part - freedom. freedom, freedom - this is through choice. everything is harking back to choice, choice, choice. freedom and choice. you can choose. you can choose. you choose your free will. you have this ability to choose whatever you want to choose and this is freedom. you can choose anything you want in this world. freedom and release. you feel that you are bonded to these things, you are bonded to life, you are bonded to these different things. you can feel them. you can feel them. you can feel them. yes, allow them [the things holding you down] to release. when you allow them to release you allow yourself to choose a different path - you choose freedom. you allow yourself to become one with Love. and this is what we mean by freedom.

when you become one with Love, when you choose to allow yourself to move outside of these obstacles that you have placed in your way. yes. we are saying you, you, you. you choose whatever you see around you. you choose whatever you feel bonded to. you choose whatever holds you down and makes you stay where you are, versus choosing moving forward. you choose this. so when you are choosing to move beyond these systems. yes, you will have to come back to them and you will have to look at these things that you have allowed to bond you and you will have to release yourself from them. *release yourself and choose to move beyond them. choose freedom. choose to frame your mind in a place of love and choose to look upon these things and see them for what they are. rather than obstructions, see them for what you have created them in your mind and in your environment.* yes, this is good heather, yes. **when you see them for what they are and you see them for their clarity. you will be able to move through them. you will be able to look at them and you will be able to see them and you will be able to move through them. when you move through them, then you allow yourself to move into a different direction - move into Love, move into Love, move into Love. choosing it, choosing Love. this is where freedom comes in.** *everything comes back to Love. everything comes back to choice. everything comes back to that. and when you are conscious of these choices and you are conscious of what is going on around you and in your environment and you are choosing a place of Love - you are choosing freedom. you are choosing freedom of choice. you already have, but you are choosing it in the realm of Love and you are choosing to move beyond these barriers that you have put in your way to move to your Divinity. this is freedom in your Christed-State. allowing yourself to reach your full potential.*

**right now most of you, as heather has described it, are at the tip of the iceberg. what you can see right now is only the tip of the iceberg.** there is 80 to 90 percent of you under the water still, that you have not allowed yourself to see. you have not allowed others to see. you know it is there. you know its there. you know its there. because it is under the surface, but you do not allow others to see this. you do not allow them to see your beauty. you do not allow them to come into contact with this because you are afraid. you are afraid and you have also allowed social constructs to control you. to tell you that this: these things that you feel that are the real you, the inner spirit, is not allowed to come out because it must be controlled by these walls, these walls, these walls - we must break these down. you must choose to break these down. they are here because you have allowed them to be constructed in your mind. when you allow yourself to move beyond that and choose Love - you do not have to go to battle with these things. this is not what we want. this is not what we want. we want you to give energy to the Love. energy to The Light. we do not want you to battle these things around you that are controlling you, that you have allowed to control you. when you are choosing Love, you are choosing yourself - you are choosing your Divinity. and these walls you will move beyond. you may have to face them and see them in the physical reality. you have to choose Love when you see these things. then you are also choosing yourself.

(devon's voice) when you are choosing yourself, you are choosing to move beyond these things. when you are moving beyond these things, you will feel the frequency. feel this frequency of Love and fill yourself. and this is what we are saying. this is what we are saying. this is what we are saying. you are choosing to move beyond yourself. you are choosing to move beyond these physical realities. this is also seen when heather does the figure 8 (explained in chapter eighteen) and she allows herself to move back and she sees the figure 8 moving across her body. she allows it to flow - the energy to flow. the energy to flow. the energy to flow. when she does this. when she sees this, she is allowing herself to back away, to see, to see, to see, to see everything is distant from thyself. everything is distant. when you are seeing these things [objectively] you are allowing yourself to pull away. and when you pull away you see that yourself, your inner soul, is projecting the thing outside of you. and when you see that those things are outside of you. you understand that you can move beyond walls. and when you allow yourself to move beyond them that is when you have freedom. choice, choice, choice. choice, choice. you must know that you are in your choosing. you are in your Knowing. and what we mean, also by your Knowing, you are in your Christed-State, you are in your Divinity, you are coming from a place of Love. you are choosing from your inner self. you are choosing from this place of Knowing. you know this thing.

*i think we have already discussed this before, but we will discuss this again. your place of knowing is to think of a time when you knew something was going to happen and you knew something about someone without it being told to you. Knowing is also truth at a Divinity level. everyone has had that at least once in their life. think back to that time and allow that feeling to come in, to be somewhere in the chest area.* yes, yes, yes, you will feel this here. and you will be in your Knowing. and when you are in this state of knowing, you know what is going on around you. you are in a state of Love. it is connection to Love. allowing yourself to be in your Christed-State. this is Knowing, this is truth, this is Love. yes, yes, yes. all of these things are surrounded in Love. Love is all and Love conquers all. this is what we have said several times before. this is what we are saying again. everything comes back to Love. all the good things, all the truth, all the honesty. all the beautiful things in life come back to this place of Love. and you must allow it. you must allow it. you must allow it. when it is flowing through you and you see things, you will see them differently. you will see things outside yourself. you will see what you are making. what you have out-pictured in your life. and you can see them for what they are. you do not allow them to affect you on an emotional state. you allow yourself to separate from them and come into your Christed-State and then project Love to these things and change these negative situations that you have created in your mind.

this is what we are saying when you need to change your life and when you need these freedoms and you need to move beyond these things that have controlled you and have brought you down to this level. and this is what we are talking about with the net of fear. you have allowed it to come over you. and when you have allowed it to come over you, come into this state where you are blinded and you feel that everything is affecting you. you are allowing things to come into your system that you have already created and then you are allowing them to affect you. you are not realizing that you are the one in control. you are the one in your choice. you can choose. and by choice you have freedom. you can move beyond these controls. you can move beyond the things that you see around you; that you do not like and discern that you do not like them. do not give them energy, because that is only going to attract them into your life.

give Love to the areas that you love, to the beauty, to the things that you want, that you choose. this is what we are saying freedom, freedom, freedom. freedom of choice. freedom to choose Love. when you are choosing Love, when you are choosing your Christed-State you are choosing your higher Divinity - you are choosing your future. you are choosing your spirituality. you are choosing everything good in this world and it will come back to you. and it will come back to you through others and through yourself and this is what we want. we want you to get away from this veil of fear and this is how you do it. this is how you do it. through freedom, through choice, through Love. and this what we want you to understand: everything is achieved in Love and through a state of Love, that you want in your Love. the true gifts, the happiness - this is received through Love. not through things. not as everyone thinks here, especially in the united states. everyone thinks that it is through gifts and through materialistic values and this is not what we are saying. this is not Love. this is objects, this is desire for object - that is not Love. we are talking about the unconditional love. the puppy love, as heather calls it. to love a dog or an animal so much, and you can feel that love and you are giving that love to the world. to everything good out there and you are allowing yourself to embrace those things and continue to love them. and that will over-ride a hundred fold anything negative. yes, we want you to understand this: you may have negative thoughts, you may see things that are negative. but if you choose to turn away from them and not give them energy and instead choose to think about the Love, move into that space of Love, flow and energy of Love then you are allowing yourself to be Love. and choosing Love (end). and choosing freedom from these things that you think are so important. freedom from the materialistic things. freedom from peoples' thoughts about you and whether or not they like you or not. these things you are moving away from them. you are moving into your power and into your state of Love and this is where you will see the world differently and the world will react differently. we promise, we promise, we promise. (pause)


## Out-Picturing


yes, this is good heather. we want to continue. we want to continue. (pause) *okay what is it that you want to talk about?* (devon's voice) we want to talk about out-picturings of life. yes, yes, yes. we want to talk about the out-picturing again. we want people to understand that everything they see in this world is at a vibrational level. where they live. who they work with. what they drive. what they don't drive, all of these things. money. lack of money, the house they live in, the people they are with, the family they are with. they have chosen this and this is an out picturing of what they have wanted in their life. yes, we are saying this: they have chosen their family, they have chosen their body from a very early stage in the spirit world. they have chosen where they are in life. they have chosen the things that they will be taught. we want them to teach themselves these things and in a faster pace and allow them to come into their Divinity. this is the time. this is the time. this is the time. it is a tidal wave that is coming, coming, coming. it is the shift in the paradigm. it is the shift in conscious thought. it is the shift into Oneness and everything that you see.

the out-picturing of life that you see has been created from you. you are the creative source for everything you see out there. so change anything that you don't like, by choosing the things you like and loving those things and ignoring any of the things that you think are bad. give love to those people that have hurt you in the past. and those people will love you or they will move on to a different life and not be a barrier for you (end). this is what we are saying. this is what we are saying. this is what we are saying. when you go to battle and giving these barriers negative energy and fight them, you attract them into your life. we are saying, instead, that you give these things that are coming up to you love. as you choose it, as you choose it, as you choose it. these barriers may come up, these people may come up and they are testing you to see whether or not you are truly choosing the state of Love. when you are choosing the state of Love, when you are choosing this, you must give them love, give them love, give them love, give them love. compassion, compassion, compassion for things, for situations, for people, for everything that you may come across that you may feel negativity towards - that you may feel as if you are not in congruence with. allow yourself to come into a Loving state. (devon's voice) allow yourself to come through these things through Love and they will come and they [negativity] will disappear in your life and you will see nothing but rainbows and sunshine we promise. we promise. we promise. it will be great. it will be great. it will be great. this is what we are saying. when you see these things coming up, you move through them in a state of Love. you are moving through in this energy source and you are allowing yourself to work through this. yes, heather we want you to talk about what you are seeing. right now. yes, yes, yes:

*so basically they are showing me this, sending me, not a super clear image, but an image of these blockages. they are almost like these black blockages whether people, objects, a wall, barriers, that we or i create in our lives. and allowing yourself to flow. when you are in this flow, you are in this energy source and it's white light and you are allowing this to come through people and when you are allowing it to come through people, beyond that is this light. this eden - this beautiful place and you are allowing yourself to let this energy flow through everyone around you and then you are walking into this eden. and these people can either choose to come with you or not. but they almost become invisible they fade away. their energy fades away from blocking you. and you come into this state of Light, into this state of Love and you feel this. if you are getting this, you feel this release in your system. you feel this removal. you feel this sense of freedom. you can fly. you can do anything you want. so if you are reading this and you are coming into this state that is perfect.*

*also, is there anything you want me to have them visualize?* yes, yes, there is. there is. there is. we want them to do the same thing that you are visualizing. visualize anything that would be blockages, barriers that you can see in your life. whether they be social, government, people which you think holding you down, your job, your spouse, your friends, your family, your religion - any of these things. anything, anything, anything that you see, that you see and you say, "i can't do this. i can't do that because of this, that, the other thing." (end) allow yourself to look at those things, see them for what they are. see in front of you now. see them around you. then allow yourself to look at each one of these things and give love to those things. say all the things that you love about them. the things that they have done for you or the things that they have done for other people - see the goodness in them. you can see the Love in them and then give them Love. you give them forgiveness if they have harmed you in any way and you allow them to be released and you are seeing this heather, now, as a release in your system. you are watching everything fade away as it turns into Light. these black objects turning into light and everything around you being washed in beautiful Light and it's surrounding you and you're coming into this state of Oneness. this state of eden. this state of Love. this peace. this Knowing. *yes, yes, yes, i see this guys.* yes, this is very good. we want people to be able to do this. this is great because they will allow themselves to move beyond these things and move into another state. there are all sorts of different examples of this through different books. but this one we think will hopefully do well for you and will help you. it is different from other ones and it will be good. it'll be good. it'll be good. *alright is there anything else guys that you want talk about?* no. this is it. we can say goodnight for the evening. thank you. stop. *name of the Father, Son, Holy Spirit. amen.*

# Chapter Seventeen

## Flow

Evening of March 5, 2013

yes, heather we are here. we are ready to begin. we are ready to come through your system. there you go. yes, yes, yes, that allows us in. yes, allow yourself to relax and allow us to come in. this is good. this is good. this is good. yes, we want to talk today. we want to talk about the book. discuss many things, many things, many things. we still have much to discuss; the book is almost there. but it is not quite done. *how close?* we are thinking about a couple more days of information that needs to be added. and then you will need to add your information in. you already know this. you already know this. you already know this from all the dreams and things that we have been sending you. yes, yes, yes. you need to allow yourself the time that is necessary to think of all the things that you want to add into this book and then add them in. add them in. add them in and then we will go over them together and then we will correct anything that we see is necessary to be corrected. this will be good. this will be good. this will be good. only a couple more days and we should have this completed. *so, what by the end of this weekend?* (pause) in a couple more days.

*alright. alright, sounds good. so what do you guys want to talk about tonight?* we want to talk about the flow. yes, yes, yes, yes, we want to talk about the flow. we want to talk about the flow. we want to talk about energy. we want to talk about how things flow together. as you are noticing, as you are shifting in your energy field that you are noticing everything flows, everything flows, everything flows. everything comes together, everything flows into one another. everything is moving. everything is vibrating. everything is moving at a different rate and things seem solid but they are not. they are not. they are not. everything is moving. everything is moving. everything is moving. this means that everything is pliable. this means that you are creating. it means that you can change it. you can change it, you can change how you feel. you can change what you see. we worked yesterday, we worked this morning. we worked yesterday too with moving through these barriers that you are creating in your life and seeing beyond that. seeing into your garden of eden, seeing into The Light and moving through these [walls/barriers], moving through these, moving through these.

yes, yes, yes. so we want to continue on this path. we want to talk about the flow. we want to talk about the flow and how it is important to yourself to open up your chakras as you have been throughout. and it is important for the reader to open up their chakras. they will be able to allow themselves to come into this energy source and into their feelings and realize they are in a vibrational state. yes, yes, vibrational state. they are part of the vibration and they can choose what is going on around them. they are conductors of what they see going on around them. and they choose to see different things. and they choose to allow their emotions to rule them in many cases and we want them to allow themselves to control this. and through control and through the place of control which is in Love. allow yourself to love everything and choose Love and you will see nothing but Love. nothing but Love. nothing but Love and this is flow. this is what we are talking about. things are flowing when things are moving. this is what people are talking about now. when they are like, "oh yeah this is flowing. this is the way this is supposed to work. this is flowing. [everything is moving smoothly]." this is coming from energy. this is coming from Love. this is choosing to be in congruence with whatever is going on and you are choosing Love. you are choosing to move through it and you are choosing to enlighten yourself to it. this is what flow is. yes, yes, yes. this is what flow is. so we want people to realize this: they can create flow with anything. they can allow themselves to connect with anything. and if they choose to love it, allow it to come into their system and to connect with it and it will come into their system and it will come into their system and be a connection as part of them. yes, this is good heather. yes, we want you to continue:

*yes, so when they are connecting with these things around them; they are choosing them into their system and they are ignoring all the things that they do not like, that they do not like and they are moving into the things they do like. and in this way they are a magnet and they are pulling these things into their system and they are pulling them closer and they are pulling them in.* you are talking about yesterday. yes, yes, go ahead and talk about this heather:

*yesterday when i was talking with my mom we were discussing how when you are driving you are gaining on someone and you are focusing on that person in front of you. say it is on a one lane road and you are thinking, "oh i am going to have to pass them because they are not going as fast as i am." and you are slowly gaining, slowly gaining, slowly gaining. finally you get to an area where you can pass them and you pass them and it seems like they are light years behind you (and there is a sense of release/ relief) and you never had to worry about them ever anyways. well this is the same thing with choosing your flow and choosing to move the things you like. often times you put barriers, we put cars on a highway of life as barriers in front of us which we have to go around and manipulate through and sometimes we get stuck behind for a really long time. and this is where we want you to just open your highway and allow yourself to move forward. when you are looking off into your beauty, into the scenery around you and you are focusing on that rather than on all of these things getting in your way. you are focusing on the beautiful drive and the wonderful ride.*

*using this analogy for life: focusing on the beauty, the life, the gorgeousness, everything around you that you love - you are focusing on those things rather than the barriers in your life. you are focusing on choosing to free your highway. you're choosing to open up the lanes and allowing yourself to flow into this beautiful world and connect with it and moving the barriers - the cars in your way and have a free ride. allow yourself to flow. allow yourself to drive comfortably through your life and enjoy everything that is going on around you. because when you are in love with it, everything is in love with you and everything is just beautiful. so this is one of the things we talked about the other night and i thought it was a good analogy for what they were talking about which is flow. let me see what else they have to talk about here.*

yes, this is good heather. yes, yes, yes. okay yes we want to continue on with this. this is exactly what we are saying. (devon's voice) you must align your chakras and get them all working and you must get them balanced. you must allow yourself to come into this. their are different ways. different books you can read on how to do this. this is up to you. this is up to you. this is up to you. you must choose the information that you are going to bring into your system. often times if you are looking for it - it will be brought to you. and this will come into your life and you can choose it. and you can choose to understand it. heather is working with her energy system, which she did not understand before. she did not understand the flow. she did not understand the chakras. she did not understand this. she understood that she had a connection with us and she understood that she could reach that connection. but she wasn't so sure how she could do it. now every single time that she comes into this state she allows her chakras to open up. fill up her space, allow them to circle around the world in her minds eye and allow herself to be connected with everyone and everything and allow it to all be interconnected because everyone is interconnected. everyone has these same chakras and everyone is already flowing together. if they choose it. they must break down these barriers and allow themselves to flow. this is what we are saying. not only is this a highway and a path of your life and what is going on with you. but it is also about other people. this is also about the world, this is also about the One Consciousness. the One. the One. the One. the One. you must understand this. when you are coming into this One state, you understand that everyone has everything that you do. they function the same way. their energies flow the same way. they may not look the same. they might not act the same, but they all have the same function. you will understand this. everyone is One. everyone is One. everyone is One.

everyone is choosing to become One on their own path [terms]. everyone is in the fast lane, the slow lane, or they are just stuck on the side of the road. this is up to them and you must allow yourself to move forward in Love and then others can follow your same tracks. they can follow your same highway. they can follow your same Light. so this is what we are saying when some people feel like they need to beat other people, or tell people, "hey you are not doing this right or hey you're stuck. hey, hey, hey,

hey." well the only person that can get themselves unstuck and get their car back on the highway and moving forward is themselves. so if you are the beacon of Light at the other end of the tunnel or at the other end of the highway and you are making fast passes and you are moving past these people and they choose to align with you, because they like this, they see what you are doing, then they will move forward. and as they move forward; you will continue to move forward. but we do not want you to think that you are being held behind by these people (or that you are superior to them because you are moving faster). so do not allow yourself to tangle with the energy source that is there. allow yourself to be the beacon of Light. allow yourself to move forward. allow yourself to make new paths on this highway and allow yourself to be unique and be you. be The Light and share it with other people.

this is how you do it: you are the lighthouse and you must be the beacon of light for everyone to see. when you do that, you allow them to come to you. you allow them to connect with your energy source, with your Light and move into the flow, into the traffic flow and come into this next level that you are at. yes, there are people beyond you. yes, there are people behind you. yes, yes, yes, yes. so we are saying, focus on you and then allow the other people to come to you. this will be part of the flow, part of the Love.

so this is very important. people do not realize that they must allow themselves to focus on themselves. and this is very different in this society (for some). this society does not believe in focusing on too much of the self, because this is considered "evil" and ego-centric and this is not what most people believe is good in this society. however there is a certain level of you that you need to focus on. you have a self worth to yourself. you have to love thyself in order for others to love you. in order for you to move forward. in order for you to connect with the flow.

allow yourself to flow. this is very important. this is very important. this is very important. we want people to realize this is: what you must do in order to move forward. you must allow yourself to connect with this and to connect with the flow and move forward.

(pause, end devon's voice)

yes, we are ready to speak. yes, we are ready to come through you. you can feel the change in your voice. yes, yes, we are coming through you at a much higher level. we are able to come through you because you have allowed us to. you have visualized it. we are here. we are here. we are here. we are ready to talk. we are ready to talk. yes, this is good. this is good. yes, we are coming in at a different level than what you have experienced before. and this is okay. this is okay. this is okay. we are here at a higher level so that you do not have to think about it as much and this is what you wanted. so we are here to do this. if you choose not to, you can allow us to not. you can put up barriers. this is up to you. this is up to you. this is up to you. good, heather. now you understand. you can choose. you can choose. you can choose. you can choose.

we want to continue on this path. yes, on the path of flow. yes, we want to continue on this path of flow. yes, we want to continue to talk about it. we must discuss this. yes, this is important. flow is major to love. flow is a major part of Love. flow is important. you must allow yourself to come into congruence with this and there are many different ways that you can choose to do this. and we have discussed some of them. allow yourself to come into your imagination. allow yourself to visualize these things. allow yourself to connect with the energy and allow yourself to move into this system. when you do this, you are becoming

part of the flow. you will feel yourself connect with all of
the things being said in this book. and you will be able to
move into this system and be able to move into the flow.
and this is what we are talking about. yes, yes, yes. this is
what we are talking about. we are saying you can move
into the flow, whatever you choose. you can do this now,
you can do this this evening if you want.

    yes, yes, everything around you. everything around
you is part of the flow, is part of the Love. it is a part of
everything that you could ever want. everything is a living
organism. you look at things and you think they are solid.
you think that they are dead. you do not think that they are
there to speak to you. everything is living. everything has a
source, a flow, an energy and this is what we are saying.
**the trees in your back yard which you think are there to
provide you shade or they are there to provide ambiance
or whatever you think about these trees. they have
energy, they have flow. they have life, they are all part
of the Oneness. everyone around you is part of the
Oneness.** everything has a spirit. everything has a soul.
everything has an energy source. and when you are
connecting with the things that you love, you are pulling
them into your energy source and you are bringing them
around you and you are allowing them into your life. you
are allowing them into your out-picturing. you are allowing
them into your system. and they connect with you and they
vibrate with you and they continue to go with you. so if
there are things that you do not like, you must look at them
and you must decide how you will change them. you must
focus on the flow. you must focus on the energy. you must
focus on where the energy is best placed. where it must go.
this is important. this is important. this is important. this is
important.

(pause)

*what else do you want to say?* we really have nothing else to discuss tonight. we realize that you are tired. we are working with your energy system to get you in alignment with us. you are very close. you are very close. you are very close for us to come through you much more easily. for you to not have to focus on the information coming through and then have to translate it, as you see it. it is coming through you. but it is not. you are filtering this information through you and you are reviewing it before it is spoken. so it is draining your system and we understand this. so we will work with this system overnight and we will attempt to get it to where it needs to be for the morning. so we say goodnight to you. we love you our child. we love you our child. we thank you very much for your time this evening. we are so excited for this to almost be done and we are so excited for others to read this and connect with this information. you are a beacon of Light. you are a beacon of Light. you are beacon of Light and we love you. *love you too.* amen. *amen. name of the Father, Son, Holy Spirit. amen.*

# Chapter Eighteen

## Chakra Flow

Morning of March 6, 2013

*okay, some thoughts just went through my head, "we are who we choose to be." which is if you don't like what you see in the mirror it's because you are choosing not to be happy. if you don't like who you are, well then this is because you are choosing not to like who you are. you are choosing to do something which is not in congruence with who you are - your true self, your Divine Self. so this is something that you have to choose to change, and choose to see a different outlook on things. this is all part of the choice factor and your view and your perspective. once you understand that your perspective is what your world is, you can understand that you can change your world. okay let me open my chakras and see what they have to say.*

*another thing, when you think about the infinity sign going in front of you, going up and down and passing through your heart chakra and reconnecting everything. that your center is your heart, you start thinking about that, and this is also like the mixer. it makes everything flow together so you are not thinking that these different chakras are not interconnected. they are interconnected and you are giving them flow by visualizing this. my mom has noticed improved digestion and so have i. it is actually very interesting, if you begin this, how your body reacts to this.*

yes, heather we are here. we are ready to speak. we have much to say. today is going to be short. we are going to say a little bit, because we know you have to leave. we know that you have to get ready and we do not want to put too much pressure on your system to get this out and get this going in time.

yes, you just discovered flow. and you are seeing flow through your chakra system. this is good. this is good. this is good. we want people to understand there is flow in many different ways. and there are many different understandings of flow. flow is the energy; flow is connecting to the energy. but flow is also in you. **you must have flow in your system in order for you to realize that everything comes back to the heart - everything connects to the heart. everything. mind, soul - everything is connected in with the heart. and once you realize this then you realize everything is connect through Love.** yes, everything is connected through Love. everything comes through Love. everything is a part of Love. and everything comes from the source of Love. when you see that everything comes from the source of Love, the heart is the center of everything around you and everything is infinite and everything comes from infinity. and everything around is always and will always be. just as this world will be and everyone here is always and will always be. just as this world will be and just as the spirit world will always be there. (devon's voice) people will always be here. this is what you understand. you understand that by realizing this infinity and realizing that you come from the source of Love and that you are a source of Love and that this is your centerfold. this is who you really are and what your energy system is computing and always come back to and always centering on. you realize that if you are coming from this place you are coming from your center and you will not be off-center.

yes, you are a libra. so you understand that you are always trying to balance yourself. balance yourself in different areas of your life and come back to your center. well Love is your center. Love is everyones center. if they choose to center themselves, if they choose to become whole. if they choose to use all dimensions of themselves, then they realize that they must come from the place of Love. and when they come from the place of Love, they understand that they are One with everyone. because everyone is using their center source. everyone comes from this place. everyone is in flow and everyone is in Love. and this is what we are saying: everything comes from Love, everything will return in Love. Love, Love, Love, Love. flow. flow yourself into this section, flow yourself into Love. flow yourself from this place. allow yourself to open up. allow yourself to be all that you can be. allow your true spirit. allow the rest of the iceberg to come up and float above for everyone to enjoy and everyone to come to as a beacon of Light and as a beacon of Love. so when they realize this, that they can come from this place of Love. they will. they will. they will. they must choose it. they must choose it. they must choose it. this is up to them. you can only give them information, heather, through this book and you can only allow yourself to continue on with your teachings and continue on with the learning from this book and applying this information into your life and others can do the same. and they can realize where they can go and what they can do. when they come form this source of Love, nothing is unimaginable. nothing is unattainable. everything is there for them to choose. for them to have.

there, of course, are some things that they may not choose from [attain] because they do not fit their life style, their Love. they do not fit who they are and what they want and these things. and we understand that that is why there are many different things out there for everyone, and they must choose their Love and they must choose what they Love and this is perfect. (shift to jamaican accent) and when they are choosing to come from the source of unconditional love. infinity. the true Love, the true place of this. they will choose everything correctly for them and for anyone else around them, because they are choosing for the Divinity, they are choosing for the Christen-State, they are choosing for Love. yes, yes, yes, yes. everything will be lifted. this fear net has already been lifted in place of many things. and [Love is] coming into you when you are sourcing yourself into flow and you are allowing yourself into the source of Love. you do not see this net. you do not see these fears. they do not interrupt your life, they do not come into them. instead you are focusing on your flow. you are focusing on your duty. you are focusing on moving forward and flowing into your true self and your true path and what you truly desire.

sit now, in yourself and allow yourself to be calm. allow yourself to ask your inner self, your higher self, what it is that you truly want. ask your Divine self now, what it is that you truly wish for on this earth and be silent and allow this answer to come. we are doing this with heather, right now. let us continue. (pause)

you desire helping one another and you desire unity, you desire balance, you desire beauty, you desire perfection, but most of all you desire peace. peace in your knowing. peace in your loving. peace in your caring. peace in your life and this is what you want. *and is this book a path to that?* (end jamaican accent) yes, this book is a path to that heather. yes, of course it is. you are choosing your Divinity when you are choosing this book. you are allowing yourself outside of your comfort zone. you are allowing yourself to come into your Divinity and you are allowing yourself to come forward. and this is what we want. you are dropping your veil of fear about many different things. about being put down by people. about being seen as a freak by people. yes, you are allowing yourself to become One and allowing yourself to be your true self. and allowing others to choose this for themselves as you have chosen. this is important. this is why this book is being written because we want others to realize that they can have this too, at any age, and they can choose this and they can be One with this. and this is what we want. this is what we want. this is what we want. so yes, this is part of your Divinity. this is part of your Divine choice. this is what you truly want in your soul and you are choosing it and you are moving forward with it.

*huh. well that's good to know. okay. so should we continue on with the book?* yes, we should yes, yes. (jamaican accent) okay, yes. so, we want you to have chosen this. we want you to have done this experience. allow the answers to come. allow them to flow through your system. do not block and do not think, "ehhh i am making this up in my mind." just allow them. most likely they are peace, help, wanting to unite people. this is common. this is what everyone wants because they want unity. they want to become One. they want to move towards this source of being One and then through this they want perfection. this is one of heather's, she wants perfection - this is attainable. everyone thinks that perfection is only in the eye of the

beholder. yes, it is. so if you believe yourself to be perfect.
if you choose to be perfect, then you can be and you are. so
you must allow this and not worry about it. everything is
perfect in it's own way. (end) even if you think they are
flawed, this is your choice to see the flaws. this is your
choice to be flawed. this is your choice. but when you are
choosing perfection you are choosing Love. you are coming
from the source of Love. everything is in Love and
everything is perfect. and we are saying things now. this is
what we are moving for. this is what is coming about. this
is what is happening. you are all moving towards this state
of Divinity. towards this state of Oneness. towards this
next consciousness. towards this next paradigm, you are
moving there. you are moving there. you are moving there.
we are making leaps and bounds to get you there. it is time.
it is time. it is time.

*okay, is there anything that we need to talk about this
morning.* no we think this is it. we understand that you need
to leave. so we will stop for now and we will allow you to
go and do the things that you need to do today. allow
yourself to relax. allow yourself to enjoy what you do today
and then come back to us later. we will continue on with
this chapter or with another chapter. we are unsure yet. we
will decide. we will decide. we will decide. *okay sounds good
guys.* we love you my child. we thank you for your time.
and we wish you the very best and allow yourself to enjoy
the beauty around you. we love you. we love you. we love
you. we love you. *thanks, i love you too! amen.* name of the
Father, Son, Holy Spirit. amen.

Notes After the Channeling Session

*we are infinite beings. we are infinite creatures. this means we have
all of eternity. we are infinite. we can get all the things done that we
need to get done in our life time, in our soul path and not have to*

worry about them - they will be done. they will be completed. so this really allows us to focus on the now. we don't have to worry about, "i have to get this done. oh my gosh, the world is going to end." no. you can get things done when you need to get them done. they will all come about and they will all work out. so don't worry so much about that. focus on the now and relax, come to peace. a great quote on facebook by lao tzu, "if you are depressed you are living in the past. if you are anxious you are living in the future. if you are at peace you are living in the present." so when you feel anxious or depressed come to the realization that you are not in the now. and then focus on the now. allow yourself to just enjoy and then you will be able to enjoy every single moment after that because you are creating a flow. you are connecting into your heart chakra. you are connecting with the source of Love because you are relaxed. you are at peace. you are in Love with this moment. this here, this now.

okay so something else that i just thought of, is when you know someone disrupts your energy field and you feel like, "oh my gosh. i should get back at them some how." it is because you are reacting with that energy you just received and you are allowing that energy to come in to your system. so instead, think of it this way: you are putting up a better barrier and you are allowing yourself to work through these things through Love, rather than trying to get back at them. be the bigger person, as they say. when you are choosing Love. you are choosing to move through the state of disruption. you are choosing to allow your system to learn from what just happened and you are not giving back to them more of the same energy and then attracting it back to yourself. whatever you give you get back in return. so just allow yourself to come from a place of Love, which is sometimes hard to do.       this is also the same concept as turning the other cheek, from Jesus' teachings. and just allowing yourself to Love. if you are coming from a place of love consistently, these people can't get into your system of energy. so in a way this is a warning sign that you have dropped your energy system. when you're outside of Love or not centered through Love. so that you can feel and be effected by these lower frequencies. if you *are coming from a place of Love, all you can receive is Love. so just continue on, even if something comes into your system and bugs you - choose Love. things will heal a lot faster. you will move past them. it is much easier, trust me. this doesn't mean that you let someone walk all over you. when you are coming from a state of Love. Love is very powerful. Love reaches into other people and Love is felt by other people, they feel ashamed usually of their actions. and usually don't do those same thing again. they are also learning through the state of Love when you choose Love. choosing Love is not only beneficial for you it is equally beneficial for the other.*

# Chapter Nineteen

## Source and Flow

Evening of March 6, 2013

we are here heather. we are ready to begin. we only have a couple more chapters and then we will be done. so you are very close, very close, very close and then you will need to add your information into here. you know what this information is. any of the notes you have taken, any of the side stuff previous to this. we want you to take these notes and add it into the book. yes, yes, yes, yes. we want people to connect, connect, connect. not only with you, but with us. this is a relationship. we want people to understand that this is a relationship and if they choose to speak to their guides this is also a relationship. so this is very important. this is very important. this is very important.

the mission of this book is not necessarily how to

connect with your guides, but instead about how to get to The Light. this is a guide on how to get close and become The Light. and yes we do want it to be called "the closet channeler." yes, heather. we do. we do. we have evaluated. this is what we have decided. so yes, this is to say the closet channeler and then we want it to say a guide to the light. and then we want you to be on the front. it is not only your visualization, of what you think. you kind of think that you make these things come up. but this is also us. this is also us. this is also us. (devon's voice) we come through you, we also see these things and we decided that they are good for you and we project these images to you as well. this is co-mingled together. this is a creation between both of us. and we like this. we think this is good. this is good. this is good. *should i mention you guys in the book, you know like devon and the 27? i am getting no answer on that you guys. any thoughts...*yes, yes we think this would be good. yes, yes go ahead and mention us in the book. you do not know a lot of information on us. we just want to bring in this information that we have brought forward. yes, there will be more books. yes there will be. but this is the one to start off. so this is okay, we don't want to have a whole bunch of information about us because you have not discovered all of us yet. you can mention and talk about us in the foreword if you choose. we do not care. we do not care. we do not need honorable mentions or anything of that nature. we understand that this is different from this world and your world. we understand that there is a difference between this world and your world. your name will be on the book. we want this. we want this. we want this. you can choose to have us on there, but this is up to you. this is up to you.

*okay so what should this chapter be about?* this chapter we are going to continue on flow. we are going to continue discussing flow and you have noticed different things about flow. you have discussed when you are driving and people get in to this sense of getting into each other's space and they understand each other's space and go into the flow. and when the flow is disrupted, this is when aggression or other things happen. and we want you to understand this. this is true in life. we are using these car examples because most everyone can relate to these things. and so we think they will be good for everyone to think about. when you are driving and you are kind of pacing the car in front of you and just going through life. usually when you are pacing the car in front of you everything is in flow, everything is moving around you. everything is beautiful. you are usually looking off at the scenery and you are just allowing yourself to enjoy the moment. you are allowing yourself to relax in this moment. and this is good. this is good. this is good. yes, yes, yes. we think that this is a good flow. so we are saying now imagine that someone just cuts you off, just comes around you and just cuts you off and then all the sudden you have to slam on the breaks or you speed up to try and not allow them in - which ever way you choose. there are many different ways that we have seen it done *(I laugh)*. so we want to say there is uhmm...that when this happens you are out of flow. you get caught off guard and all the sudden you have a challenge in front of you. and now this is what we are saying you can choose to meet this challenge in different ways. choice again. we are coming back to this thing of choice. always, always, always. choice, choice, choice. so we are coming back to this and we are saying that you can choose to be aggressive. you can choose to honk your horn, flip them off. do whatever you think is necessary in order to get their attention and realize that you are mad at them. you can bring this energy into yourself and it will stick to you. you noticed this earlier, yes, the sticking of the energy to you. so then you can do that approach and you can also

do the approach of, whatever i don't care and back off
again and relax. this is different. you can choose whatever
you want. you can be ticked off at them and hold onto that
energy and allow it to become part of your system and
allow it to become part of you and then you are out of flow
and instead you are focusing on this barrier again. you are
focusing on it with so much energy that you are giving into
it and allowing it into your life or you can allow yourself to
back off and come into the flow again and allow yourself to
come from a source of Love. if you do not allow them to
affect you. they will not be able to effect your system.
sticking their energy to you and creating more of this
violence in your system.

this is an analogy for what you do in the real world.
this is how, when you are in flow. you are in the beauty.
everything is going, everything is wonderful. you are
whistling while you are walking or whatever it is. but all
the sudden a challenge comes up and meets you in the face.
you are going to have to decide, what it is, what you are
going to do. are you going to back off and not engage with
that energy and let it go on by and focus on the beauty all
around you? or are you going to put all of your energy into
this thing and give it all that you've got and try to force
your way through it and try to tell them how ticked off you
are and give them all of your energy? and then at the end
of the day, all that you are is upset and unhappy. you can
choose. which do you choose? we know that there is an
aggressive competitive nature, especially in this western
culture. we understand this. we see this very competitive,
"have to be going in front of the person and i can't allow
them around me because then it seems like i am a loser or
something." this is silly. come from the state of Oneness. if
you are coming from the place of Love, you no longer care
if someone beats you. it doesn't matter. there is no beating,
there is no winning. there is just you. allowing yourself to

relax in the state of Love. and if they choose to do that, as well, then you are always in your state of Love.

so we are saying that we have approached this before. yes, heather you are questioning this. yes...we have approached this before. we have said that if you are in the state of Love then you do not have these [negative] things pop up all the time. yes, yes. we are saying this is true. but we are saying initially when you are getting engaged with this, little barriers, little challenges will come out and test you as to whether or not you're going to truly choose the path of Love. this is just the way that it is. think of it as a game, if you will, and this is the competition. so your competition, instead of choosing to be aggressive and showing what a big man or woman you are and how amazing you are through your ego or whatever the situation may be - you choose to allow it, to let it go. when you let it go, it flows away from you and you flow back into the source of Love and you are in the state of beautiful wonder and allowing yourself to once again swim through the beautiful life that you have - nice and easy and enjoy everything around you. and enjoy the beauty that is unimaginable when you are in the state of Love, because you have not experienced it before. many people on this earth have not experienced it. except for maybe a couple times. and they can maybe hark back to this and understand that it is real and they can choose this at any time. they can choose to be in love with themselves and then in love with the rest of the world at any point in time. you can choose it now. so we are saying this is up to you: you must choose, you must decide what will work for you. yes, yes, yes.

*okay guys, that was good. what else do you want to talk about?* we want to continue talking about this. we have another example. it is not totally related. it is about the worldly flow. we want to get out of the context of just being in this country. we want you to understand that just because there are these barriers now, we want to think broader: the barriers of languages, the barriers of cultural differences. these things just because they are...these barriers, you must not allow them into your system. when you allow yourself to flow and realize that everyone is One. that everyone can feel the same energy and know who you are and you can know them and feel who they are and feel their energy - then yes, you understand that everyone is One. everyone can feel and be One. we may not be able to speak all the same language. this will come. this will come. this will come. you will be able to move beyond these barriers. you will come to point where you can telepathically speak to one another and language barriers will not matter. this is coming. this is coming. this is coming. this is not now. so we are saying things are moving forward. things are going to happen and this will become easier. but you have to allow yourself to realize this is not a barrier. embrace the beauty, embrace the flow of the world, embrace people around you - everyone is One. just because they have different colored skin, different colored eyes. different colored hair, different ways of behaving, different views on some things, different souls (as you see them) - you are all One. you must choose the flow. what flow do you want? if it is the flow of Love, then you choose everyone and you choose it for yourself. you choose this and then you allow it into your system and this is exactly what we want. we want people to come into this and realize that they are all One and they all inter-connected. and none of these religious beliefs, political beliefs, any of these beliefs really matter. because when you are all One, you all come from a place of Love and you can learn all of these different things. this is up to you. this is up to you. this is up to you.

(pause)

yes, yes, heather you realize the pressure on your head this is very good. it means that you are allowing us in more. you can feel us coming in. you can feel our energy coming through you much more easily and it is because you have allowed yourself to actually open up your crown chakra much much more than you have ever had before. and this is very good. this means that you are allowing flow to continue. you are allowing yourself to flow. and we have already talked to you about the chakra flow and this is very important to allowing yourself to be in Oneness and to see yourself for what you truly are, which is very beautiful.

## Source

*okay so what else do you want to talk about with this chapter? or do you want to continue on with another chapter?* (pause) yes, heather. yes we want to continue on with another chapter. this chapter is going to be called source. yes source, heather, source. this is going to be called source. this chapter is very important. it is about The Source; the source of Love. the source of all things and where this comes from because people wonder - people wonder. they wonder where everything comes from and this is for whatever reason very important. people must know Source in order for them to understand it. so yes we are saying you are The Source for everything. you are The Source for your universe. you are The Source for life. you are The Source for what you want to see in this beautiful universe or for whatever things negatively. so you choose whether or not it is beautiful or not. you are The Source. you are The Source of energy. you are The Source for your universe. as they say you are the center of your universe.

and this is very true, whatever perspective you have, whatever upbringing you have, whatever things you cling onto and hold to be true and set as parameters around your life, what you see and what must be, this is what you are - The Source. so you choose this.

right now we are making a symbol with heather of a rectangle. yes heather, "L, L" with the hand switched upside down and the hands flaring. we are saying this is part of The Source and allowing your energy to flow and this is what we are doing with you right now. yes, yes, yes. we will come to this in a minute. we must allow you to keep doing this and then we will discuss it. *okay sounds good...is this like a doorway?* in essence yes, this is a doorway. this is a doorway for you to continue forward and for you to move through. you can feel the energy coming through the center and you can feel it building. yes. yes, continue heather. yes, continue. we will discuss other things while you do this. *okay sounds good.*

so yes, we want to speak of The Source and yes, yes, yes, lets get back to The Source. lets get back to our topic. it is very important that you understand everything comes from The Source. everything is One with The Source. everything must be part of The Source. so when you are choosing things, you are choosing life and you are trying to understand things. everything comes from you. you are worried about this God, this omnipotent person and whether or not he is going to judge you. He is a person, She is a person of Love. there is no such thing as sex, there is only such thing as a Being and they are a Being of Love. He, She whoever you want to say is God. God is a being of Love and God is here for everyone. so yes, we want you to understand this. this is very important. everything comes from this place of Love. everything is a source of Love and when you realize that you come from this place of Love, then you can realize that everyone around you also comes from the place of Love. we talked about the well of Love. yes this is part of The Source. yes, everything. everything in this universe comes from Love - everything. we are saying things that you think are bad and the things that you think are good, everything comes form The Source of Love. we are not talking about peoples actions, we are talking about objects. we are talking things in this world. we are talking about the ocean, we are talking animals, we are talking about children, we are talking about plants, we are talking about everything of this sort of nature. and these things and they are coming through and they are part of The Source of Love. this is what we are saying. everything comes from Love and everything is part of Love. and when you understand this, you understand that you are The Source, and when you are The Source, then you can be anything you want to be and true love - this is all possible. so you must continue. you must allow these things of Love, this place of Love and come from it. yes, yes. this is The Source. this is The Source for the world. this is The Source for continuing on in your life path. this is The Source. everything flows through energy. everything flows through it. and The Source of energy comes from you.

you are the conductor of energy. so you can choose whatever frequency you want to be on. we have also heard this is the radio, you are the radio and you can choose what frequency you want to bring forward. do you want to bring forward the source of negativity darkness, things of that nature? or do you want to bring forward The Light and Love that is around you always? and by choosing the beauty and by choosing these things you will be the broadcast for everyone else and they can tune in. yes, yes we are saying the radio comes to the actual broadcaster. yes, yes. you can choose this. and you, as you choose it, as heather is right now. she is choosing The Source. she is choosing to be part of the Love and she is choosing to be the radio and bring it forward and as she is the radio, as she gets this book done and as she gets it published she will become the broadcast. and this is what we are saying. she can be the broadcast and you can be the broadcast. this is something she will bring about later. *this is something you can do, i can do it.* this is the sense of unity we want the world to understand. you are all One. you can do what your brother and sister does. you see something you like, you can do it as well. there are no limitations in this world; except for the limitations in your mind and the limitations you put forward. so you are free. you are part of The Source. you are part of the Love. so you must choose this. if this is what you want to bring forward. this is up to you.

yes, heather. yes, yes. you are still wondering what is going on with this gang sign as you are thinking about it in your head. yes, yes, yes. this is a sign that we want to be brought forward, this may go on your cover. you will see. we will tell you later what this is meant to be and you will see this later. and right now we want you to continue doing it and understand that you are connecting to the flow of your body. everything is moving through this source right now. we are working with your energy and this is why we are having you do this. this is not just some random thing that we are having you show and having you do. this is the connection. we want you to realize that both sides of your body connect together in The Source. everything is connected. everything works together. just as you believe it does. we are working with your energy right now and allowing this to happen. yes, yes. you are just thinking whether or not you should look this up. feel free to look it up. you may find this symbol somewhere else and it may give you more insight. we will share with you in time what this means. but we will not right now. and this is okay. you are okay with this.

*is there anything else with The Source that we should be discussing? i just feel like it should be a little more infinite than that. but maybe it is just me.* no, no, not tonight. we are good, everything is good. this is the end of this chapter for right now. we are saying there may be more added onto this. but for right now we are going to allow you to just relax. yes, yes. yes, this is very good. allow yourself to relax. come into the state of consciousness. into the state of being. into the state of relaxation. very good heather. yes, yes this is very good.

(pause)

yes, you see heather, yes you do. you see the link, your hand. yes, yes you do. see how people share their energy through touch and this is what you are seeing through this connection. you are seeing the hand shake, you are seeing many things about the hands and as they come together. yes, yes, this is good.

(pause)

*is that what you guys are saying about this?* yes, heather, now you understand. yes, very good. yes, yes, yes. we are saying this the window through which you see, just how little you see. you see them only through your fingers as a window. but yes the whole world, it is out there for you to see. yes, yes. this is what we are saying. this what we are saying. this is what we are saying. connected with the flow. you must allow yourself to realize this is, what you are seeing. this is how you have limited yourself and you can move beyond this, you can move beyond this symbol. so choose to move beyond. choose to move beyond. choose to move beyond these fingers. choose to move beyond. choose the tree of life. choose The Source. choose yourself and

choose the beauty and love around you. yes, the symbol.
yes, you understand now what it means. yes, it means this
is the window through which you see and beyond is all that
can be seen. you have limited yourself, but now it is time to
move beyond. it is time for everyone. they must realize this.
they can move on. they can choose to move on. this is up to
them. this is up to them. this is up to them.

(pause)

*is there anything else we should talk about guys?* no,
heather we think this is all. it is time to discuss the rest of
this tomorrow. yes, you are good. we are ready to stop. we
thank you very much for your work. we appreciate
everything you have done for us. this has been a beautiful
night. you have gone through much of the material that we
wanted. *so how many more days or anything like that on this?*
couple. yes, a couple more days. yes, yes. you are almost
there. you are very close to being completed, as far as with
our channeling and then you will need to do other things.
yes, yes this is right heather. yes, you will need to do things
after this. but we want you to continue channeling in the
morning and in the evening until we get this done. we are
very close. we are very close. we are very close. *okay sounds
good guys.* we thank you very much and we love you my
child. *amen.*

# Chapter Twenty

## Source of Light & Love

Morning of March 7, 2013

*a couple things i was thinking about with the window expression. couple things you can be hands on with your perspective. your perspective is all yours. it is all part of what you choose. you can take snap shots of different things and be further out and see only little bits of things and miss a bunch of life or you can bring your focus inward on your Source, on your Love and see everything. and see everything for what it is and not have any barriers. so this is something to think about.*

let us begin. we want to begin by talking about. source. we want to discuss source. we want to come in and we want to discuss source today. yes, we want you to continue discussing this picture that we showed you and the things that you have inside your mind. yes, yes, with the hands. yes, we want you to continue discussing it. yes, what you

were saying earlier is very good. yes, yes, you have a
control on where you set your picture frame at. you have a
control on what you see. you have a control on what you
allow to come into your life and connect with you on an
energy level. you have your own control. so we are saying
this. if you choose to see things further away and you chose
to see them from a distance then you are choosing this. you
are choosing to only see a little picture of things here and
there and you are not choosing to see the whole picture.
this is how many of you are. many of you take snap shots
of different things and you say, "oh this must be my life.
this is the way it must be, because everyone else is seeing it
this way and everyone else is doing it this way. therefore
this is my life." but this is not true. your life comes down to
what you want to see. what your perspective is and what
you want to see. you can also see this with other people.
there are people that you can't stand, in some cases,
because they only want to see the world through what they
want to see it through and you want to shake them and go,
"hey! why cant you see what i can see? why aren't you in
alignment with what i can see?" because they are choosing
not to be. and this is okay. people choose many different
things for themselves. they often times choose it as a lesson
to themselves and they often times choose it from a state of
fear, control, or safety. this is what they want. they want to
feel safe.

anything that you think is safe out there is coming
from a state of fear. and when you are coming from a state
of fear, you are not seeing the whole world for what it is.
and this is what we are saying. you have to come from a
place of Love. and when you are coming from a place of
Love you see the world. you see all the colors, you see all
these people in it and you see the beautiful vibration of the
world in which you are living in. and when you come from
this place you are connecting with the One. you are

connecting with the One Conscious. you are connecting with everyone. you are allowing them to decide whether or not they want to come in and speak with you in a place of Oneness, in a place of Love. you are becoming that source of Light. you, by choosing to take the frame (which has probably been out here at arms length just capturing different snap shots at different times) you are choosing to move it back in. move it in where your eyes are and allowing yourself to see the broader spectrum. allowing yourself to see everything that is going on. yes there may still be some blocks along the side frames but you are getting there and everyone is getting there. as everyone gets there the energy will shift to where the people that are getting very close to being able to see everything will be able to see it all. we must do this as a team. everyone must come together. and this is what we are saying, everyone must choose this.

everyone can choose this in their own time. time is something that you all think is very important. well it isn't. you have as many lives as you need to get to where you need to go in life. so do not worry. be in the present. enjoy it. when you are putting forth that energy, here, now, others can do the same and this will change your future. your future is from here forward. it is from what you choose right now. you are projecting forward. you can change the next moment which will change your future and the next moment which will change your future and the next moment which will change your future. so we are saying if you choose to be in Love and you choose this for here, for now, for always. you are choosing the best and brightest future you can have. you are choosing for yourself and for everyone else around you to move into The Light. this is what we want you to understand: you are The Source of your creation. you are The Source of what you want to see. you are The Source of The Light. you are

The Source for people to come to and choose their Light and you are that source and everyone is this source. not just heather. not just paul selig, not just these other people that have come out and have connected with their guides and written books. everyone is trying to get everyone else to this level. and there are different people here that are meant to do this and their are people that will do it in their own ways. and this is what we are saying. come from your Source. come from your Love. and you will be part of Love. you will be fulfilling your Divinity. you will be fulfilling your purpose. you will be fulfilling your true desires by doing this. and this will come with peace and this will come from happiness. so this is everything that you want, you just have to realize it.

you should have already asked yourself the question and you should already know what it is that you want to do while you are on this planet. while you are here in this life and what you want to achieve, truly achieve from a Divinity aspect. often times these are broad spectrums like i want to help people, i want to bring unity and you don't know how this will be done. it will be shown to you, trust us. it is being shown to heather every single day. if you are choosing to ask and you are choosing to wonder, the way will be shown to you. the path of Light will be shown to you. each and every one of you. you are The Source for your creation. you are The Source for your future. you are The Source for your life. what do you want? you choose. you can choose anything in the world. so what do you choose? do you choose what the ego wants? do you choose the nice brand new car? do you choose the million dollar home? do you choose the wife that looks amazing or the husband that looks amazing? what is it that you choose? or do you choose to focus on yourself and have these things come to you? often as a by product of you choosing your source, your Divinity and what you are truly here to do -

because God wants you happy. we all want you happy. and
these exterior things they can make you happy, but they
are not your true source of happiness. this comes from
within. this comes from within you. this is your source. you
are The Source. you are The Source for your creation and
for your life and for your beauty. you choose it, you choose
it, you choose it. so this is always up to you. you are always
in your state of choice and this is a blessing. we are not
going to force you to do anything. no one can force you to
do anything that you do not want to do and this is up to
you. you can choose what you want. we are hoping that
these words will ring true with you. and you will see that
you truly have The Light and you have the power because
you are The Source.

so we want to say this again: you are The Source for
your creation. you are The Source for what you see. you
are your own source. you change your own perspective.
you decide where your picture frame goes. and when you
decide where your frame goes, this is what happens in your
life: you see what you want to see. you either see it all or
you see different parts and aspects. so this is very
important. this is what we wanted to discuss today: we
want to discuss this source and this is what is coming
through. yes, this is very good heather. yes it is.

(pause)

The Source, as we say, is part of you. The Source as
we say, is your well. this comes from the well of Love. so
when you are choosing this. you are becoming The Source
of a well of Love for other people. as you overflow, they
can connect with you and they can drink from you and
become a well. we spoke of this before. this is also part of
The Source. we want people to understand this: everything
is interconnected. every subject is interconnected to itself.

this is why we repeat things over and over and over again. because we want you to understand. that this world just as it is a sphere and it is connected - you are all connected - all topics are interconnected. everything is a sphere. every energy source is a sphere, everything is interconnected. your life force is a sphere. you will always end up passing away and coming back. this is what you will do. you can choose the places that you will come back at, but you will always exist. this we want to comfort you with - you will always exist no matter what. you can always choose whatever life you want. you can choose wherever you want to be. you can choose. so when you are choosing this life. you are choosing this source. you are coming to this Light and you are being the source of Light for other people. yes, yes. and we are saying that you are infinite and you continue forever. just as infinite as this earth is. just as circular as everything is on this planet. just as history repeats itself. just as people repeat their past mistakes, if they choose to. just as everyone does things in a circular motion. this is what we are saying. everything moves in this direction you can choose what path you want to be on. you can choose what source you want to draw from. you can choose what you want your view and perspective to be for others by choosing this. they of course must choose their own but they can connect with you and this is what we are saying.

*take a time when a teacher or mentor or anyone changed your view because they held a different one other than your own. it resonated with you, so you choose it. you were not forced to - you just did. this is what they are speaking of here. when you choose to be The Source and hold this view/energy, others can choose to change their view to match - this is the well of Love, the domino effect, ripple effect. it is very powerful for not only yourself but everyone else.*

   **this is very important information. everything is circular. everything has a beginning and another start (rather than an end) and everything continues through life.** nothing ends. nothing ends. nothing ends. it may seem that way to you, but it is not true. yes heather, we hear what you are saying. you are questioning the distinction of animals, you are questioning these things. you may end in a form, but you will not end as a source. so let us correct this. you may end in this form, you will end in this form, we guarantee it - in this body. but you will not end as a source, you will not end as a soul. you will continue forever. you are infinite. you have no end. you have no end. we want to say this again. you may end in this form, but you will not end as a source. you're infinite, infinite, infinite, with infinite possibilities and you choose those possibilities. you unwrap them because you want them and you choose them. and we will be here to help you as your guides to come through and help you to get you to where you need to go and this is up to you. when you are choosing things we will come down, we will help you choose things. we will give you the guidance that you need. everyone has their own spirit guides, everyone has their own ability to speak to them. yes, maybe in different ways, at first, but everyone has access to all the different parts of the psychic ability. yes, we are saying clairvoyance, we are saying clairaudience, we are saying clairsentience and we are saying all of these. you have all choice to connect with them. this is always up to you.

   many of you will remember as a child speaking with Spirit. speaking with these people or seeing them. yes, yes, yes, you will see this now. as you allow yourself to think back, think back, to what innocence was. think of the dreams that you used to have and how vivid they were. think about how crazy your life was because it was full of color, it was full of interest, it was full of Love. and when

you see this you see that you can tap into this source, as
you did then, you can do now. yes heather, yes, you want
to continue on with this thought. yes, okay, yes. so we
want to discuss this, that everyone can do as everyone else
does. if you see someone and you idolize what they are
doing, you are connecting with The Source you can do it
too. heather has already talked about this, where she
discussed what she wanted to do, to see things as paul selig
and theresa caputo do and she has done this. she is moving
forward in this, because she knew if someone else could do
it, she could do it too. this is very true, of course you can.
you all have this ability. you all have your source of
Divinity, you can choose these gifts that you think are only
gifts for certain people - are gifts for everyone. everyone
has this ability, whether they choose it or not is up to them.
yes, yes, you want to discuss the book now go ahead:

*so yes, one of the books that i read during this time was open to
channel: how to connect with your guide by sanaya roman and
duane parker. it is a great, short read, on how to open and speak
with your guides. it is written in a very easy understandable
manner. you're not questioning, what does that mean or what does
this mean. it is a great starter kit to connecting with your guide. i
thought i would mention this here and i will be leaving a list of all
books i have read in the back of the book, for anyone interested.*

yes, this is very good heather. yes, very good. yes, so
we want to continue on with The Source of Light and this
will probably be the ending of this book. because we want
you to see that this Light, the way that we had you light
the candle, this is the perspective and this is the way in
which we want to end this book by lighting the candle and
lighting The Light within you. and as you burn this candle
out you are choosing to bring The Light within you. you
have now brought the exterior light that you see in the

candle and you have brought the flame within you and you are now the source of the flame. do you understand this heather? *yes, yes, i do.* very good. yes, so this is why we started and ended with this and we want this to be as everyone has seen and we are saying this is why this is the guide to The Light. it is the guide to the exterior light and it is the guide to the inner Light. this is what we want. we want people to understand this. they are The Source for their fire. they are The Source for their passion. they are The Source for their creativity. they are The Source for their Light of their life and they can choose whatever they want.

it is time now to stop allowing yourself to be controlled by these other people and by these other things. by this fear that you believe is so important to you, that will keep you so safe. this is not true. this is a limitation. a limitation on all that you can do and all that you can choose from. you are infinite. we want to say this again. you are an infinite being of The Light. so choose your Light. choose your inner Light and you are choosing this not only for yourself, but for everyone else. choose it and become One with it. yes, heather this is what we are saying: become One with your Light.

yes, heather continue. so we want to say that this is very important. you must continue on with this. you must choose it. you must be it. and then everyone will become One and they will become One through this Light. through this source. this bright white light. this flame that flickers within. and by yourself lighting this candle every night, you are choosing to light it for everyone else and you are choosing to light it for your Source, for your inner self and you are bringing this Light into yourself. *is this something that you guys want the reader to do as they read this book?* this is up to them. you can talk about this if you want. but we want them to understand what was done while you were doing this book. so they can decide what they want to do and they can see where we are coming from. and they can decide what they want to do.

there are multiple layers into everything that is done by your guides to bring you forward and bring you into The Light. so we want them to understand this. there are many different layers. there are many different things. there are many different dimensions on which we can work with you. and so we are working with everyone and we are working with them to try and move them forward and move them into The Light and become The Source of The Light. choosing The Light and choosing the flame within. yes, yes. many people have covered this up, they have held it under a cover. yes. heather you are thinking of this let your light shine. yes, you heard this in catholic school. no longer hide your Light. allow it to shine for the world to see. allow them to connect with it and become One with it. this is The Source of Light which is The Source of Love. all of these are interconnected. and they are One, just as you are One with them. you can no longer disassociate yourself with all of these different things. you must face the things that you have chosen and you must again choose The Light and choose The Source. when you are choosing these things you are choosing to go forward in Love and you can break down any barriers. you can break down anything that you have brought into your life, that is not part of your Divinity and you can move forward. this is important.

*okay so this is the end of the book? i'm not getting an answer.* no this is not the end of the book, you still need to write your part. *do i keep on channeling?* no, we are not done channeling heather. we are getting very close to finishing this book, but we are not quite done. *okay do we have more for this session or do we want to continue onto another session?* we have said what we need to today. thank you very much for

all that you have done. we will continue on this evening.
thank you. thank you. thank you. now stop.

# Chapter Twenty One

## Magnificence

*so what should we continue with guys?* this chapter is going to be about the Magnificence. yes, you are wondering what this is. Magnificence is the aspect of God within everyone. people call this Divinity, people call it other things, we are calling it the Magnificence. we are calling this within you. everyone has this. everyone can be this. everyone can join this - they can be magnificent. they can choose their Magnificence. they can choose this. they can choose this. they can choose this. we are saying this slightly different from Divinity. it is part of the Divinity, but it is also the part of the other things, it is all part of you. we want to say that the Magnificence is what you choose. when you choose this, you are in a state of Love. you are choosing your Magnificence, you allow information. allow it to come into your system. allow it to come into your system. allow it to come into your system and you're becoming part of it and you are allowing yourself to become One with everything around you. when you choose to surround yourself with everything that is beautiful and choose to incorporate them into your life this is what we are saying is magnificent. you become one with everything and you allow yourself to do this.

you will see that your life does not need to be an escape. you do not feel like you need to escape from life. instead you can enjoy the here, the now. you are in a state of Love. so therefore you are in a state of everything that is going on around you and you choose this here, now - you choose to be part of it. and as you do this, you choose to come into a state of Love and you are magnificent. you radiate. you radiate. you radiate this Magnificence and you choose it. you become magnificent in your glory and all of your beauty which you are choosing. you are choosing to become the well of life - The Source. yes, yes, yes. you see that all of these things come together and they all work together and this is what we are saying: all words, all things, all things work together. everything has flow, everything has meaning, and it all works together. we are all working together.

(pause)

yes heather, we know that you are tired. so we are going to try to get through this information as fast as we possibly can. so let us continue with this Magnificence. yes, yes, yes. we want to connect this with The Source, with the flow. Magnificence is connecting to everything around you. Magnificence is drawing the energy and allowing it to become part of your Source. realizing that at an energy level and allowing yourself to grow. and allowing yourself to incorporate all of the things around you that you want. yes heather, you are seeing the things with the white light around it. yes, when you truly want something with all of your heart and your Love. you love it so much that you want it in your life, you put this magnificent Light around it and so we are calling it Magnificence. when you are putting the white Light around it, you are choosing to put it into your energy field, because you are choosing to connect with it and you are choosing part of your energy and it is choosing to be part of yours. this is the point of Magnificence: everything that you choose comes into this and becomes part of the flow. and when you see it, you truly have a connection with it. you have a connection with this thing and you become part of it. you become part of The Source. you become part of The Love and you move forward.

(pause)

Magnificence is oneness with God. Magnificence is oneness with the self. Magnificence is oneness with the universe. Magnificence in essence is becoming One. yes, this is another word, this is another terminology. you are questioning why we have repeated things over and over again. this is because we are trying to show that everything is interconnect - everything has a flow. (pause) Magnificence is the inner working of Light. it is how Light works. it is how it comes through you and this is the word of Magnificence - it magnifies. and it magnifies, it becomes stronger and you see the white Light around things coming into your system and you see them flowing into your system and magnetizing to you. this is what we are talking about with Magnificence, we are talking about magnetism. now we are connecting what we wanted you to connect in your brain. you see that we are bringing the information in much easier for you to understand. when we try and we repeat, repeat, repeat, it is because we are trying to break through barriers and come in. when you allow us to come straight through you, then you allow us to come in. you don't necessarily have to work with it and think on it while we are bringing it. you can sit back and you can allow yourself to relax. yes, this is good.

so we want you to realize that Magnificence is magnifying the glory, the beauty from within and allowing this into your field and then echoing this out into others' fields. and this is what we are saying: there is a radiation, there is a ripple effect that we discussed earlier. and this is what we are talking about with Magnificence - this is how this works. when you magnify things towards you and into your energy field it is because they or people or objects and things are connecting with your energy through your Loving Source and they are choosing to come into you and they are choosing to come into your Source. they have connected on a higher level. that many people do not understand yet. and they have chosen and the objects have chosen to now radiate into your field and be magnified by you. this is what we are saying when you are creating from a source of Love. when you are creating from The Source, all of these things you are magnifying, these things you are creating a magnet which is yourself and you are bringing these things to you as if you are a giant fridge and all these magnets are getting stuck to you. so we want you to realize that the things you see out there that you don't like, those you have magnetized to you. you have given them energy to connect with you and come into your life and be a bumper sticker on your refrigerator instead of being a beautiful magnet with the great wisdom on it. or whatever it is that you choose that you like.

so we are saying this to you: you have to choose the things that you want, just as we have said before. we are using this to apply the essence of The Source, and The Power, and The Divinity and all that goes with all of this. you have to come from this place of magnetism and realize you can bring anything into your life that you want. yes heather go ahead and speak about what you wanted to talk about earlier:

*so one of the examples that i wanted to bring forward is about the ripple effect. i was relaxing by myself in the still water of a large hot tub at the gym. slowly at first i was kicking my feet and not paying attention, and nothing much was really happening. the water was still, except for right around me and then all the sudden this momentum builds and it builds and it builds and the water is moving and splashing against the sides. but it took it a little while to get it to that place. it took my momentum and slowly working at something to get it there and this, i believe, is what they are trying to say about magnetism. is it guys?* yes, it is. this is why we gave you this example this evening, because we wanted you to experience this first hand. so continue with what you are saying. *so yes basically how it works with magnetism, as you know, if you try to throw a magnet against the fridge and if you are too far away, it doesn't stick. so you have to get more connected. this means you have to become a stronger magnet, on the ripple effect of love, for the objects that you want to stick to you. at first it is slow, you are sitting there splish, splash, splish, splash, thinking nothing is happening. then all the sudden the ripple effect kicks in, everything is moving in motion towards you - moving in congruence with you. it comes back and it is magnified even larger than it was before and the whole entire world is moving in this way. it is coming back to you and rippling back into you and magnify straight to you.*

*so this splish splash water effect, you can learn from this. go to a small pool and see how long it takes for the water to start rippling back and forth to you. it is actually a really fun experience. and I'm not talking really splashing. i'm talking slow rhythmic movements.*

*so at first this whole process may seem very slow and you are like, "what is the point." then all the sudden you notice things are coming about and working for you in your life. so the biggest thing that i have to say about this is: don't lose your momentum. because once you lose that, you lose the ripple effect coming back to you. so you just have to keep working through it. allow yourself to keep working through these barriers that you have set up. break through and move them. allow yourself to see your garden of eden. attract it to you through Love - through your Source. allow yourself to be filled up with the beauty of your life, as it truly is, and the self that you truly are. overflow and allow others to see this, as well. and you will be able to see this ripple effect of your life. it may be slow going at first, depending on how big your pool is and the objects you put in it. but it will happen, you will get there.*

yes, heather this is very good. we wanted this to be spoken in this book this evening. *is there something else that you wanted to say?* no, this is it this evening. we understand you are tired. we want you to get up in the morning and we want to channel through you. we appreciate your time. we appreciate what you have done for us and yourself. we will continue working with your system as you move forward. we thank you for speaking to us this evening and love you very much for everything you have done. *thanks guys, love you.* we love you too.

# Chapter Twenty Two

## Energy and Light Source

Morning of March 8, 2013

okay, let us begin. let us begin. we have much to discuss today. we must continue. *okay what's the chapter going to be about?* we are going to come back and highlight The Source. discuss what you have learned heather. discuss what you have just discovered:

*okay this morning i was just thinking about The Source and things like that. everything has an energy source and everything comes from energy. so you have to have an energy source for the energy to flow to something else. just like when you are lighting a candle you have to have an energy source, whether it be a match, a lighter, etc. so everything has to have a source in order for it to be created. people that know energy systems know this really, really well. but, once you understand that everything is an energy source and you allow your inner-self to become The Light; choosing yourself to become the candle of Love, and unity, and peace - choosing this. then others can light their candle, their inner-source from you. and then as this happens many many candles can be lit. everyone's candle can become lit. everyone can become Light.*

*but first you must have a source. so anyone can become their own source as they see it. but in reality they are lighting their candle from a greater source - God. people choose their Light, they choose their source, they don't let anything cloud it. you can see this is especially true in children. they are all bright Lights: bubbly, loving, sharing and caring. they don't think too much about themselves because they know they are loved, they are thinking about other people. so when you look at them you realize that as we become older many of us have become clouded by the ego self. we must look a certain way, we must act a certain way, we must be a certain way. it is not okay to talk to your guides. it is not okay to do this, that or the other thing. it is not okay to play anymore. we often lose the fun and the magic that is around us in this world and yet we have so much of it. when you come in contact with someone your own age still acting this way [like a child] about life you think of them as naive or annoying. we think, "well that is just ridiculous. why aren't they like everyone else, upset and unhappy with their life? why are they out having fun and seeing the magic in life. they need to grow up." you know? instead of just realizing that life is all about that - fun, magic, wonder.*

*when you are born into this life, you are born into it with having fun, playing around, talking with your guides. allowing yourself to be in the spirit world. allowing yourself to love everyone unconditionally no mater what and you are born into this. and of course you are saying, "we cant all act like children, we have to discern from things." of course and children discern from things. what they like and don't like. but they usually aren't focused heavily on what they don't like. instead they weigh more of their energy, attention and focus on what they do like. and they end up getting those things. do you notice this? even at this young age, all humans have this ability to embody The Light and they choose to focus on what they love. we have lost this and it is time for us to let our Light shine. become the children of The Light.*

yes heather, this is very good. we especially like the part about the children. yes, always watch the children. if you watch the children you can see that their ego is not clouded. that their ego has not set in, often times. they are at this place of innocence and when you watch this place of innocence you realize this is the place that you came from and you were born this way. you were born into this beautiful world, as magical and as beautiful as it is and that is all you saw. you saw people for their inner goodness. you saw things for their inner goodness. you light your Light and you focus on the good not the bad - this is where you came from. now you have clouded yourself by what you "should" be doing in society and what you "shouldn't" be doing. this is not true. this is not true. this is not true. break out of this mold and be who you are. we are not saying like the people that pretend to be who they are. they pretend because they latch onto this other group, this other class of people that are pretending too. in a way, forming in their own egotistical group and we are not saying this. we are saying move beyond these groups. move beyond these classes. move into you. do not focus on everyone else; do not focus on them. do not focus on what they are doing and everything else. do what you want to do for you. there are so many sources out there. yes you know this heather. yes, yes. continue:

*there are so many sources out there for you to choose how to be you - the Divine Self. people have been doing this for years. there is the shamanic journey through the native americans. there is meditation through the eastern cultures. there is channeling and choosing to do* that. there is tarot card reading. there is being creative in your own source. when you choose to be you, you are coming from your creative source. whether it be a painter, a writer. whether it be figuring out the next way to build something, invent something. figuring out the next genetics, discovering the next medical breakthrough. these are all part of your inner creative source; you have all of these abilities.

"you already possess everything that you need to be great." - native american, crow. you were born with everything you need to be great, to be an inspiration, to be what you need to be to be your greatness. so choose this. if you realize you are just not creative; you are not feeling creative anymore. especially if you are stuck in a rut. for example: if you are working at a office job everyday doing the same thing everyday and you don't have any time to do anything creative or you don't think you do. pick up what you used to do in high school. didn't you use to sing, act, paint, make pottery, jewelry, read books, write books or start a new business ventures with friends. this is part of accepting that you are creative again. realizing your own Source. realizing the real you and allowing this to flow through you.

when i went to the Medium in sedona, she said that i needed to become more creative and that my creative chakra was shut down. i was no longer being creative. i was no longer doing these things. your creative chakra happens to be your throat chakra. so i was like, "i have to get creative, you're right. i haven't been doing anything in a long time." so i started journaling. i started reading. all the things that i did when i was younger and home schooled and also in high school when i had time. so i started doing those things. i decided i was really into the native americans right then. so i picked up a beading kit and started beading. i really liked all these pictures of native american people and i just really wanted to show the beauty of native american people to this world. so that was kinda part of the creative source and you have to connect with and just come into it. and now when i think about it, opening up my throat chakra is exactly where i channel through.

*so all of this came through* **channeling, channeling, channeling.** *your guides will have you do things that you will be like, "what? why do i have to do that?" like lighting the candle. i think i have talked about this earlier. they said to light my old baptismal angel candle every night until it was burned out and that is when i would be done channeling the book. so i simply thought this is all that it can be. but of course not. then they explain that this is lighting your inner Light. and this blew me away. i was like, "wow! i totally didn't know where that was coming from, but that was cool." they will shoot information into your brain and you will be like, "wow! that has meaning to me. that has power. i am going to use that in my everyday life or share with the world through a book." never let yourself forget those moments or ignore those moments of instant enlightenment. they are coming to you for a reason. realize those are from your guides or your higher self.*

*coming back to the Oneness, people are connected outside of this world. people who have passed over, people in other planes, people that are here now. the grasses, the plants, the birds, the trees - everything. we are interconnected. everything is One. which is perfect and beautiful in its own way. let's see what else they have to say.*

this is good heather. yes, we are ready for you to begin. we are ready for you to begin on your journey, on your path and on your information for this book. so we are ready for this information to get typed up and allowing it to flow through you and allowing this book to be developed. *wooohoooo!!! thanks, love you!*

# Conclusion

in conclusion of this book, my guides have asked that i share some information on how i work through these concepts they have presented and share notes to my discoveries along the way. as well as, my perspective of the experience of writing this book with them. i have presented much of this information in the preface and in the following sections:

## MY TAKE-AWAYS

i am learning to take a step back. be in the now and see things objectively. when you are looking at the world through Loving eyes, you are objective and non-judgmental. you remove yourself from giving energy to the things you don't love and instead you focus on all that you do love. reminding yourself that everything has a place in this world. as benjamin franklin once said, "a place for everything and everything in its place." we must learn our own worth. everything and everyone on this earth has a place and it is in its' place for a reason. this again, everything in its' place and everything has a place for a reason. this book, for example, has a place on this earth and in certain peoples hands and it is already there because you chose it.

i am constantly reminding myself that i am in my choice. we can do all that we want to do. we are the ones who limit ourselves. bring your perspective, your "frame," into close view and see the world for all of its' beauty. open your mind to all the possibilities. they are just as infinite as you and i. we are truly blessed by our freedom to choose and we should never take for-granted that we have our own choices to make. we have power through these choices. "whether we think we can or we think we can't, we are right" - henry ford. we can choose to be One or we can choose to be separate as we have in the past. it is up to us to choose. that's the beauty, you can choose to believe what ever you want to believe. ask yourself, are you happy with what you have chosen and where you are now? no? then don't be afraid to change and experiment. this is something that will change your life forever. this world is here for us to explore, make mistakes and learn. we are the children The Light and like children it is time to have fun and play as we did before the rules set in and life became a job rather than our playground. sure we have to live within the laws of the universe, but we can make them work for us as well. take an airplane for example, a hundred years ago we could not imagine flying through the air like a bird, because of the law of gravity and lack of wings. now however, it is a reality and we can't imagine our lives without the technology we have around us today. if it wasn't for the wright brothers experimenting, dreaming and choosing to believe, along with those before and after, we would be stuck on the ground still. remember by choosing The Light you are choosing the brightest and best version of yourself. it is up to us, all of us. the young, the old, men, women, children, all religions, all races, all versions of the human race to choose - choose to unite. choose to be the truth - we are One. let your Light shine all of my brothers and sisters. no more fear, only love.

## MY LIFE TODAY

my life has changed in many ways since i first verbal channeled my guides. to date, i have been talking with my guides regularly: while i drive to work in the morning, finish this book, watch tv, etc. their presence is a constant reminder that we are never alone and this world is far different than I believed it to be a year ago. i find great comfort in their loving presence and friendship. as of late i have asked my guides to present themselves to me every single night, so that i may get to know them individually. so far they have proven to be an interesting group. perhaps the next book will be about meeting my guides. one never knows.

other than channeling daily, i spend much of my time with my family and daughter, as well as running the daily operations of my parents' hot tub store. i have enjoyed that these new found psychic abilities have brought our family closer together. my mother and i talk daily about different things we have read and discovered on various topics related to the psychic world. it is a blessing to have such a loving and supportive family to share this new adventure with.

my wish for the future, is to bring people loving and truthful information. which will propel them into their own Knowing of themselves and their true worth. This book is just the beginning of my mission and adventure. I look forward to sharing more with all of you in the future. Until then, live your life full of fun and laughter, be present, and my The Light be with you.

HEATHER HUNT
July 29th, 2015

# Additional Material

## BOOK LIST

*Embraced by the Light*
by Betty Eadie

*Auras: How to See, Feel & Know*
by Embrosewyn Tazkuvel

*The Secret, The Power, The Magic*
by Rhonda Byrne

*I Am Word, The Book of Love and Creation* (Channeled Texts) by Paul Selig

*The Science of Getting Rich*
by Wallace D. Wattles

*Awakening to the Spirit World*
by Sandra Ingerman and Hank Wesselman

*Open to Channel: How to Connect with Your Guides*
by Sanaya Roman and Duane Packer

## YOUTUBE VIDEOS

*Michael Newton - Souls and the Spirit World - FULL INTERVIEW*
by vyperius
http://www.youtube.com/watch?v=NnCr4etOZLw

*Waking Universe: Paul Selig & I Am The Word*
by WakingUniverseTV
http://www.youtube.com/watch?v=Z7BI0Lgb9Kk

*Your words and thoughts have physical power - Will Smith*
by Mark Sansom
http://www.youtube.com/watch?v=Z7BI0Lgb9Kk

If you would like to stay in touch, please visit my website:


www.theclosetchanneler.com


Offering, FREE Secrets to the channeling community and Get Psychic: ways in which to test your innate psychic abilities. Read my Blog, revealing daily insights and words of wisdom from "Devon and The 27."

Also, like *The Closet Channeler* on Facebook and follow me on Twitter.

CPSIA information can be obtained at www.ICGtesting.com
Printed in the USA
LVOW10s1328090916

503941LV00023B/276/P

9 781491 248935